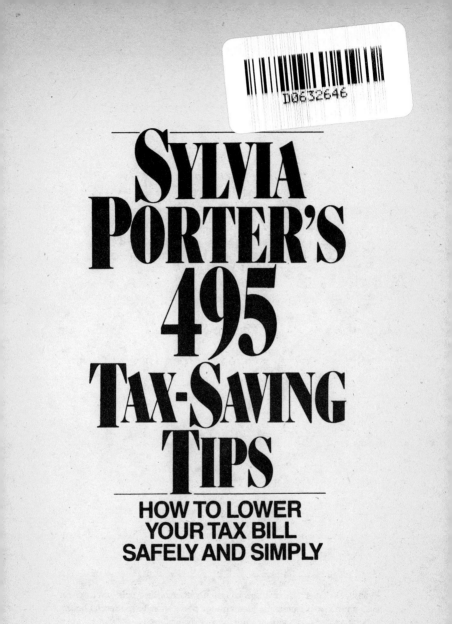

SYLVIA PORTER'S
495
TAX-SAVING
TIPS

HOW TO LOWER
YOUR TAX BILL
SAFELY AND SIMPLY

Day k.

Other Avon Books by
Sylvia Porter

SYLVIA PORTER'S A HOME OF YOUR OWN
SYLVIA PORTER'S LOVE AND MONEY
SYLVIA PORTER'S YOUR FINANCIAL SECURITY

Coming Soon

SYLVIA PORTER'S GUIDE TO YOUR HEALTH CARE

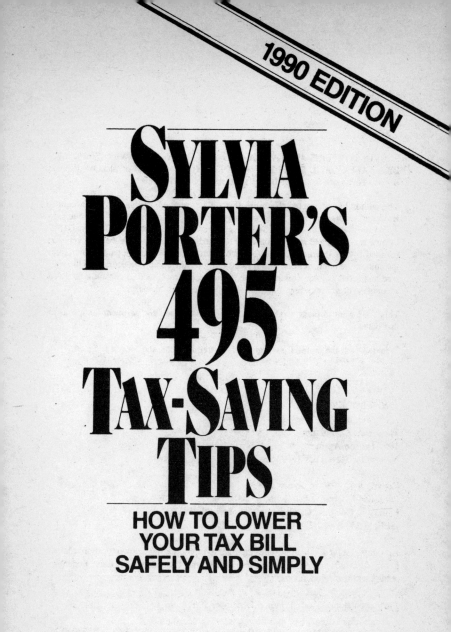

1990 EDITION

SYLVIA PORTER'S 495 TAX-SAVING TIPS

HOW TO LOWER YOUR TAX BILL SAFELY AND SIMPLY

AVON BOOKS ◆ NEW YORK

SYLVIA PORTER'S 495 TAX-SAVING TIPS: HOW TO LOWER YOUR TAX BILL SAFELY AND SIMPLY (1990 EDITION) is an original publication of Avon Books. This work has never before appeared in book form.

The author has attempted to ensure that all information in this book is accurate. However, errors can occur, rules and regulations regarding tax and other matters do vary from location to location and are changed from time to time. The final 1989 income tax forms and schedules and the updated official instructions had not yet been released by the Internal Revenue Service when this book was prepared. Therefore, the author and publisher disclaim responsibility for the complete accuracy of the text. And as is always mere common sense, the reader is cautioned to consult a qualified accountant or attorney regarding accounting or legal problems.

This book went to press on October 13, 1989 and reflects the pertinent tax law as of that date.

Prepared with the editorial assistance of Warren Boroson and Steven I. Feiertag

AVON BOOKS
A division of
The Hearst Corporation
105 Madison Avenue
New York, New York 10016

Copyright © 1989 by Sylvia Porter
Published by arrangement with the author
Library of Congress Catalog Card Number: 89-91923
ISBN: 0-380-89997-3

First Avon Books Trade Printing: December 1989

AVON TRADEMARK REG. U.S. PAT. OFF. AND IN OTHER COUNTRIES, MARCA REGISTRADA, HECHO EN U.S.A.

Printed in the U.S.A.

OPM 10 9 8 7 6 5 4 3 2 1

TABLE OF CONTENTS

v

INTRODUCTION

So you thought that the Tax Reform Act of 1986 meant there would be no wholesale tax changes for a while?

Alas, now we have the Medicare surcharge . . . talk of restoring the favorable treatment of capital gains . . . and much more. Changes have been so quick that even a respected newspaper recently discussed deducting mortgage interest if you use the proceeds to pay for educational and health expenses. (That tax reform innovation has already gone by the boards.)

But the plain truth is that if you want to save money, you'll just have to keep up with all the tax changes. Many people do. Evidence: The second most common reason why Americans take out home-equity loans is . . . to buy cars! (The first: for home improvements.) Obviously, taxpayers know that although interest on car loans is no longer fully deductible, interest on a mortgage is—even if you buy a car with the mortgage money.

Then again, it's possible to pay too *much* attention to tax changes. Take the Medicare surcharge—not strictly a tax,

1

but one that sure quacks like one. It's so unpopular that the rules may have changed by the time this book goes to press.

Yet the surcharge isn't universally unpopular. The securities industry—those folks eager to sell you municipal bonds and other tax-favored investments—are in seventh heaven. They want to persuade older Americans that, by lowering their taxable income, they can reap a twofold benefit: not just lower Federal and state taxes, but a lower Medicare surcharge.

But, for many people, trying to avoid the surcharge would be dangerous and even costly. I'll explain why in Chapter 1.

Another major new development: congressional activity to lower the capital gains tax. The possibility of a lower tax has led homeowners to postpone selling their houses and investors to defer selling their profitable securities.

THE SINGLE BEST TAX TIP

"If there's a single best tax tip," Arthur Harris, a CPA in Boca Raton, Florida, tells me, "it's 'Learn to keep your tax records together, so you don't forget or lose anything. And you needn't fumble around for vital documents when you or your tax preparer need them.'"

THE LATEST CHANGES

Here's a brief rundown of the changes that the Tax Reform Act of 1986 wrought, along with other recent changes:

• Starting on January 1, 1990, you can buy Series EE savings bonds as a neat way of saving for your children's college educations. The interest you receive from bonds issued on that date or later will be nontaxable when the proceeds of the bonds are used to pay for college tuition and other educational fees.

Here are the rules:

1. The proceeds of the bonds must be spent on tuition and fees at a qualified educational institution. Included are most accredited colleges, junior colleges, and certain schools of nursing and vocational education.

2. The tax exemption is available only to the buyer of the bond, or to a spouse or dependent of the buyer. The buyer must be at least twenty-four when purchasing the bond. If the bond is to be used for the educational expenses of the buyer's child, the bond must be registered in the buyer's name.

3. Only interest used for educational expenses, like tuition, books, and laboratory fees, will be tax free. The rest will be taxed proportionately. Example: You cash in $10,000 worth of bonds, of which $5,000 is your original investment and $5,000 is interest. If you pay $8,000 (four-fifths) to an eligible school for tuition, you could exclude $4,000 (two-fifths) from your taxable income. And you could exclude another $5,000— because that's just a return of your principal. You would pay taxes on $1,000 of your interest.

4. The tax break is phased out for families with adjusted gross incomes (AGI) from $60,000 to $90,000 when the bonds are cashed in. (See the definition of "adjusted gross income" below.) For singles the tax break is curtailed when their AGI is between $40,000 and $55,000. The phaseout is proportionate, so that a couple with $75,000 in AGI would receive half of the bond interest tax free. These income levels will be adjusted for inflation as the years go by.

• In certain circumstances, you can add the investment income, over $1,000, of children under fourteen to your own income on your own return. This will save you from filing a return for your child and some complex calculations. You'll need Form 8814.

• If you take the child- and dependent-care credit, you must provide information about the provider of care.

• If homeowners are physically or mentally incapable of taking care of themselves and spent time in a state-licensed facility, they are still eligible for the $125,000 exemption of gains when they sell their main home—if they've lived in the home for a total of at least one year during the five before they sold it. (The usual rule: three years.)

• Those insurance contracts when you paid in money, then quickly got a loan, have been restricted. They're now called "modified endowment contracts," and you face an additional 10 percent tax if you withdraw too much money too quickly.

• "Like-kind" real estate exchanges, where you trade properties and may thus defer paying capital gains taxes, *may* be severely curtailed. The House Ways and Means Committee is recommending that tax-deferred real estate swaps be limited to properties "related in service or use." That would mean no more tax-free trading of a store for an apartment, a farm for a condominium, and so forth.

• There are now only three tax brackets: 15 percent, 28 percent, *and* 33 percent. (See Appendix A for the new tax tables.)

• Capital gains are now taxed just like ordinary income. For 1987, the maximum tax on long-term gains was 28 percent, even if your last dollars of income fell in the 38.5 percent bracket. For 1988 and now for 1989, your capital gains—long-term or short-term—are taxed like ordinary income, which means that they could face a 33 percent bite.

• Home mortgage interest is generally fully deductible if you obtained your mortgage before October 14, 1987. After that date, you're limited to $100,000 plus the balance of the debt you incurred to buy and improve the home. Top limit: $1,100,000.

• Personal or consumer interest you pay—on credit cards, auto loans, and such—is only 20 percent deductible for 1989. Such interest will be 10 percent deductible for 1990, or perhaps not at all, and certainly not at all deductible for 1991. These "phaseouts" are all over the place, but fortunately they tend to follow the 40-20-10-0 sequence.

• The standard deduction climbs to $5,200 for married couples filing a joint return, to $2,600 for marrieds filing separately, $3,100 for singles, and $4,550 for heads of households.

• The personal exemption climbs to $2,000.

• The maximum amount of earnings you must pay Social Security on climbs from $45,000 to $48,000 for 1989, with a $7,209.60 maximum ($3,604.80 each paid by the employee and the employer). For the self-employed, the maximum is $6,249.60.

• To avoid penalties, by April 15 taxpayers must have paid 90 percent of the taxes they owe through quarterly estimated-tax payments or through withholding from their salary checks—or 100 percent of the taxes they paid the previous year.

• Creative artists—writers, painters, artists—can now deduct their expenses in the year incurred rather than over a three-year period, regardless of when they receive the income. (Under Tax Reform '86, those expenses could have been claimed only when income from the work began coming in.)

• Personal service corporations will be taxed at a flat rate of 34 percent, rather than the three-step system of 15 percent, 25 percent, and 34 percent. These corporations are those formed by accountants, lawyers, doctors, and other professionals.

• For 1989, losses from "passive" investments are generally limited to 20 percent of the amount those losses surpass profits from passive income. This applies to investments made before October 23, 1986.

Bear in mind that now there are three kinds of income: (1) active income—what you get paid from your job; (2) passive income—what you receive from renting out real estate or from participating in a limited partnership; and (3) portfolio income—what you receive from stocks, bonds, and other securities.

The distinctions are important. Generally, you can't use losses from passive income (tax shelters) to wipe out taxes you would otherwise owe on your active income or portfolio income. (Naturally, there are phaseouts of these losses—and, to make things more complicated, a special exception for certain investors in rental real estate!)

BASIC TAX-REDUCING STRATEGIES

For 1989 and beyond, experts are recommending that taxpayers be flexible. All sorts of unexpected changes may be in store for us.

Just keep firmly in mind what Justice Learned Hand once said: Tax avoidance isn't the same as tax evasion. You can do everything within your power to lower your taxes, by legitimate means. You can sell stocks that have gone down, to get a tax loss, then buy the same stocks back (thirty-one days later). You can buy municipal bonds, just so you won't have to report any interest. But you may be guilty of evasion if you take a loss on those stocks and secretly buy them back within thirty-one days—or if you never report the interest on savings bonds you've cashed in. "Avoidance" is legal; "evasion" isn't.

BUNCHING. Throughout this book, you will be told about a perfectly legitimate tax-avoidance strategy. It's called "bunching." It means pushing, or pulling, your deductible expenses into a target year.

The reason bunching has become so important: You may lose deductions unless you have enough of them to surpass a minimum amount—a "floor."

Example: Before you can deduct your medical expenses, you must first be able to list all your deductions ("itemize") on Schedule A, which is part of Form 1040. That requires that all of your itemized deductions add up to more than the "standard deduction" you're entitled to. (There's a glossary at the end of this introduction, in case you're unfamiliar with any terms.)

Today, only your total medical expenses that surpass 7.5 percent of your "adjusted gross income" can be deducted. The 7.5 percent is the "floor."

For casualty and theft losses to be deductible, you must first subtract $100, then your losses must surpass a floor of 10 percent of your adjusted gross income.

For a variety of other expenses (certain "miscellaneous" deductions), there's now a floor of 2 percent.

What you do when you bunch your deductions is to try to have all your expenses surpass a particular floor in a particular year.

Let's say that next year (Year 2), you plan to move to a new job, across the country. Your new employer won't pay you for the cost of the move. You can deduct the moving costs only if you qualify to itemize. Otherwise, none of the expenses will be deductible.

What you should do is try pushing your other deductible

expenses from Year 1 into Year 2. That way, you're more sure of being able to itemize in Year 2.

For example, if you receive medical or dental bills in December of Year 1, pay them in Year 2. You can add them to your deductible expenses in Year 2. If you pull deductible expenses from Year 3 into Year 2, you'll also boost your chances of being able to itemize in Year 2. Pay December's bills from Year 2 in December. You'll also want to consider pulling income scheduled for Year 2 into Year 1, and pushing income scheduled for Year 2 into Year 3. For example, if it doesn't make much difference one way or another, sell a stock for a gain at the end of Year 1, or at the beginning of Year 3. That way, your adjusted gross income in Year 2 will be lower—and (a) you'll be more likely to be able to itemize, and (b) you'll be more likely to surpass the floors for deductions that are based on your adjusted gross income.

In short, this strategy calls for bunching as many of your deductible expenses as you can into one favorable year. But keep in mind that there may be complications: Your income in Year 2 may unexpectedly shoot to the sky (you might win a lottery). That means your adjusted gross income may rise, and so would all the floors you would have to surpass!

DEFER INCOME/TAKE DEDUCTIONS NOW. Another strategy— an old and honored one—that you should generally follow may conflict with the bunching strategy. But you should bear it in mind: Defer income, and take deductions now. The theory is that the longer you put off paying taxes, the better off you will be.

Now let me explain the postpone-income/take-deductions-now philosophy in more detail.

Let's say that you've acted as a business consultant, or painted someone's house. The company you consulted for, or the person whose house you've painted, could pay you in December of Year 1, or January of Year 2. Choose January of Year 2. If you chose December of Year 1, you would have to pay taxes on that income by April 15 of Year 2. If you chose January of Year 2, you wouldn't have to pay taxes on that income until April 15 of Year 3. That's a whole year's grace! (But remember: You may have to pay estimated taxes on that money.)

Take deductions early for the same reason. If you're selling a stock for a loss, other things being equal, do it in Year 1. That will lower the taxes you'll have to pay on April 15 of Year 2. If you sell in Year 2, you'll lower the taxes you must pay in Year 3—and may get a tax refund a whole year later!

The point is, it's almost always better to have money sooner rather than later. Money has a "time-value." The sooner you get it, the more valuable it is. If you receive money in January of Year 1 rather than January of Year 2, you could put it into a savings account and earn an entire year's worth of interest. Or you could buy a new VCR set with the money, and enjoy the device for an extra year.

USING THIS BOOK

Here's how this book is organized: Chapter 1 is a special chapter on the Medicare surcharge. Chapter 2 and Chapter 3 lead you through Form 1040, with money-saving suggestions on what filing status to choose, how to lower your reportable income, ways to take advantage of credits, and so forth. Chapter 4 plunges into Schedule A, itemized deductions. Chapter 5 focuses on deductible medical expenses, Chapter 6 zeros in on casualty losses, Chapter 7 spotlights charitable contributions. From there, we go into more detail on various investments—securities (stocks, bonds, and such), insurance-based investments, and real estate (Chapters 8, 9, and 10). Then there are detailed suggestions for homeowners

(Chapter 11), employees (Chapter 12), entrepreneurs (Chapter 13), parents and divorcées (Chapter 14), and retirees and people planning for their retirement (Chapter 15). Chapter 16 is devoted to the alternative minimum tax, a special tax for people who take advantage of too many tax breaks.

Appendix A gives the tax rates and tax tables for 1989.

There's some overlap in the book: A suggestion that someone who is self-employed hire his or her child is suitable for both parents and for entrepreneurs. A suggestion that you turn your hobby into a business could go into the chapter for employees—or for entrepreneurs. That's why you shouldn't only look at the chapter titles. Also study the detailed descriptions of the chapter titles, and check the index.

DON'T BE INTIMIDATED

Granted, taxes are just as complicated as ever. Still, perhaps you can do you tax return yourself—if you have the time, if you have the inclination.

First, it will save you a tax adviser's fee. Second, you'll probably try harder than anyone else to shrink your tax bill. As the truism goes, no one cares more about your money than you do. Third, you'll keep up-to-date on the tax code— and thus in the future be able to make sure your financial dealings take best advantage of the tax rules. If you're worried that you might make mistakes, for yourself or against yourself, you might do your own return, then have a tax preparer look it over.

Even if you do turn to someone else for help, this book can help you. Check that your preparer has thought of all the tactics and strategies mentioned in these pages. That will serve as a good test of your preparer.

Just to boost your self-confidence, here are some true stories of what other taxpayers have tried to do:

• A Connecticut man sold his house, planning to invoke the one-time capital-gains exclusion of up to $125,000 from his profit. He would be fifty-five by the end of the year. The man had $90,000 of gains. Amount excluded: zero. You must be fifty-five on the *date* of sale, not by the end of the year. In this case, the closing took place ten days before the man turned fifty-five.

• Patricia Burton, an enrolled agent in Gates Ferry, Connecticut, knows people who have built new, more expensive homes within two years of selling their old ones— but were disqualified from deferring their gains. Reason: They had not *occupied* their new homes within two years.

• Almost ten years ago, a wealthy woman in her eighties had a tax service figure out her taxes. Her adjusted gross income was $56,000, and she owed $3,000. When the tax preparer offered to help her fill out her check, the woman said she didn't have her checkbook with her, and would return home and mail it in. The tax preparer told her to use the figure on the last line of page two.

The woman returned home and sent the IRS a check for the last figure on page one: $56,000. That was her adjusted gross income, not her tax liability.

A few weeks later, the IRS notified the woman that it was crediting the overpayment, $53,000, to her next year's tax return. (When the woman's tax preparer learned about it, she saw to it that her client's $53,000 was refunded.)

• A couple, married for ten years, had never filed a joint return, even though filing separately had cost them a fortune, reports tax lawyer Martin M. Shenkman. Reason: The wife refused to divulge her income to her husband. (They wound up getting divorced.)

So . . . don't be intimidated. Try to do your own tax return; or at least lay the groundwork. A lot of other people won't do as good a job as you can do.

PREPARING YOUR RETURN

As you may have learned last year, you must start early when you're preparing your return. Don't leave everything to April 14. Preparing your return may take much longer than you had expected—especially if you find yourself missing any important documents.

In fact, to save time, you should get into the habit of organizing your records all year long.

Don't just toss all your tax records into a drawer. Sort them out before you even think of tackling your return. Have separate folders for regular income, health expenses, insurance payments, capital gains and losses, and so forth. Keep records of deductible expenses—like business trips you're not reimbursed for.

At the outset, find out what extra forms you may need. Your library, post office, or bank should have them. And to make your task a bit less difficult, buy a simple, no-frills calculator—you can deduct the entire cost if you itemize and surpass the 2 percent floor for miscellaneous deductions, assuming the calculator is used entirely for investments or tax-return preparation.

How much time you will need to do your return depends, obviously, on how complicated it is. If you don't knock everything off in one sitting, at least have a goal every time you sit down with your tax forms: for instance, listing all your medical deductions, or all your capital gains and losses. Set aside days or afternoons when you know you won't be interrupted.

Begin by recalling everything significant that happened in your financial life last year. Did a storm topple a tree in your yard? Did your landlord keep your security deposit? Did you take a course to maintain your job skills? Did you have an operation? These expenses are probably deductible.

To jog your memory, if you still have last year's calendar on which you marked appointments and special days, glance through it. Look for errands to help a charity, visits to physicians you may have lost the records for, and so forth. Naturally, you'll go through your canceled checks, your insurance reimbursement forms, and your bills, too.

Now proceed to all the income, interest, and dividends you racked up last year. Assemble your W-2 forms, bank statements, brokerage-house forms, and so forth. And gather up your bank-deposit slips, upon which you should have indicated the sources of your money. (If not, start doing it now.)

Separate your deductions into categories—medical, taxes, interest paid, moving expenses, and the like. Put your records into plain manila folders. And then plunge in—using this book to help you reduce the toll.

Remember that you can get an automatic four-month extension if you file Form 4868 by April 15 and pay what you estimate you owe. If you have a good reason, you can get another two-month extension.

Finally, remember that if you have a figure like $50.50, you can make it $51; if it's $50.49, you can make it $50.

DO YOU REALLY KNOW WHAT THESE WORDS MEAN?

One reason why taxes are so complicated is that the IRS uses unfamiliar words, or familiar words with special, unusual meanings.

If you study this list, in the future you may have less trouble understanding when the IRS talks.

Adjusted gross income: All your taxable income, minus a few "adjustments" like contributions to an IRA, Keogh, or SEP, alimony, etc. The adjustments are listed on the bottom of the first page of Form 1040.

Alternative minimum tax: A special tax reserved for high-income taxpayers who've managed to take too much advantage of tax breaks, or who are unlucky enough to get entangled in the AMT rules.

Basis: The cost of an item, when you calculate how much profit or loss you've made when you sell it. For example, for a stock, you add the broker's fee to the cost of the stock itself to find the "basis." On a house, you add permanent improvements (like a new deck) you've sprung for to the purchase price. A possible synonym for "basis": total investment.

Capital gains/losses: Profits or losses on the sale of stocks, real estate, or other assets you held as investments.

Casualty and theft losses: Losses to your property or other assets because of a sudden, unexpected, unusual event, like a storm that blew in your windows. A casualty or theft loss may be an itemized deduction from your adjusted gross income.

Credits: Amounts you can subtract, dollar for dollar, from the income tax you would pay otherwise. Example: the credit for "the elderly or the permanently and totally disabled." Credits are better than deductions. Deductions are subtracted from your income, not from your tax bill itself.

Deductions: Subtractions from your adjusted gross income. If you're in the 28 percent marginal tax bracket, a deduction of $1,000 (for, say, medical expenses) saves you the $280 in taxes you would have paid otherwise.

Dependent: Someone you support by providing over half the money he or she needs for support. A dependent entitles you to an exemption on your tax return.

Depreciation: A yearly deduction you can take on business and investment assets, like rental property, that supposedly loses value as it ages.

Earned income: Money from your job or business, earned through your personal efforts, as opposed to money from securities or from a limited partnership. Also called "active" income.

Estimated tax: Taxes you usually pay four times a year when the taxes withheld from your salary aren't at least 90 percent of the total tax you expect to owe.

Exemptions: You, your spouse, and certain dependents. Each exemption reduces your taxable income, for 1989, by $2,000. Also called "personal exemption."

F.I.C.A.: Social Security tax.

Gross income: Your taxable income from all sources. (Interest from most municipal bonds, for example, isn't taxable, so it's not included.)

Head of household: An unmarried taxpayer who maintains a residence that is the main home for an unmarried child, a dependent parent, or other dependent for over half the year. A head of household is entitled to pay taxes at a special lower rate, lower than that of single people.

Itemizing: Listing all your deductions on Schedule A, as opposed to taking the standard deduction.

Joint return: A tax return filed by a husband and wife together, combining their incomes and deductions.

Lump-sum distribution: The payment an employer makes of the balance due you from a pension or profit-sharing plan. The entire distribution must be made within one year for it to qualify for special tax treatment.

Marginal tax bracket: The rate at which your last dollar of income is taxed. If you're in the 28 percent tax bracket for 1989, your income is first taxed at 15 percent and finally 28 percent. (See the tax-rate table in Appendix A.)

Property: Real estate, stocks, a painting, a car, or any other asset (thing of value) that you own.

Rollover: A distribution from a pension plan, or an individual retirement account, that you reinvest in another pension plan or IRA within sixty days of your receiving the money.

Standard deduction: An amount you can deduct from your adjusted gross income if you don't itemize your deductions on Schedule A. (For married people filing a joint return, the standard deduction is $5,200 for 1989.)

Support: Payments you make to care for a dependent, as for food, shelter, clothing, and medical expenses.

Taxable income: Your income, after subtracting adjustments, deductions, and exemptions, but before subtracting for credits and tax payments.

Withholding: Taxes taken out of your salary to pay your Federal and state obligations.

Write-off: A synonym for "deduct" that we writers turn to when we're tired of using "deduct."

Chapter One
THE MEDICARE SURCHARGE

Should you load up on tax-exempt municipal bonds to escape the surcharge for Medicare coverage?

That's what a host of securities firms have been urging in a slew of slick literature.

The extra tax is based on the regular Federal tax bill you're already scheduled to pay, so if you can lower your general taxes, you might also lower the surcharge.

But what's in the interest of the securities firms may not be in your interest, and there's a simple argument against loading up on munis: Congress may someday decide that the interest you receive from munis will count toward the Medicare surcharge. As Paul Westbrook, a certified financial planner in Watchung, New Jersey, points out, "There's a precedent. The interest from tax-exempt municipals is lumped in when you calculate what you may owe on your

17

Social Security income. So it would only take a stroke of
the pen to make a similar change.''

So, our first piece of advice for 1989 is:

1 DON'T MESS UP YOUR PORTFOLIO IN HOPES OF AVOIDING THE SURCHARGE.

On the other hand, a great many people have virtually no
tax-exempt investments at all. Thomas B. Gau, a CPA and
certified financial planner in Torrance, California, reports
with horror having met people whose entire portfolios—$2
million worth—are in taxable certificates of deposit.

So our second piece of advice is:

2 USE THE SURCHARGE AS AN IMPETUS TO RECONSIDER WHETHER YOU SHOULD OWN MORE TAX-EXEMPT SECURITIES.

A review of the rules: Anyone who's eligible for more than
six months of Medicare Part A (hospital benefits) faces the
surcharge, which begins in 1989 and must be paid by next
April 15. (You'll bypass the surcharge this year if you
turn sixty-five on July 1 or after—unless you qualify for
Medicare because you've been disabled, regardless of your
age.)

You will owe an extra $22.50 for every $150 you owe in
Federal taxes. Limit: $800. (For a couple who are both
eligible for Medicare, the limit is $1,600.) If your tax
liability is $5,250 and you're single, you would owe a
Medicare surcharge of $787.50 ($5,250 / $150 = 35 ×
$22.50 = $787.50.)

Obviously, you'll owe a surcharge if your taxable income
is more than $1,000 and your Federal tax bill tops $150
(because the lowest tax rate is 15 percent). You'll pay the

maximum surcharge if your taxable income is about $27,300 (for singles), or $52,400 (for couples).

If you found the last two paragraphs a bit tough, be advised that one investment company, USAA in San Antonio, recently concocted the medical term "Medicareous Bewilderitis." It means chronic confusion brought on by the new Medicare legislation.

You can lower the surcharge by moving your money into tax-favored investments. A problem with this strategy, though, could be that it would be a case of the tax tail wagging the tax dog. "You should make your investment decisions independent of the Medicare surcharge," says Rudy D. Watz, a vice president and director of retirement plans for Value Line, Inc. in New York City. "If you wind up lowering the surcharge, that's just icing on the cake."

Westbrook argues that when people latch on to investments just to avoid taxes, they almost invariably wind up getting clobbered. "When investors chase tax loopholes, they may regret it later on," he warns. "Not always, but usually." A prime recent example was tax-sheltered limited partnerships.

Besides, if you're well-to-do, it's no cinch to lower the surcharge by shifting around your portfolio. This year, two Medicare-eligible people will face the limit if their taxable income is around $52,400. And if you're in the 28 percent tax bracket, you would have to reduce your taxable income by $2,357 to lower your Medicare surcharge by $100. ($2,357 × 0.28 = $660 / $150 = 4.4 × $22.50 = $99.)

If you're in the 15 percent bracket, says Steven I. Feiertag, a certified financial planner and enrolled agent in West Nyack, New York, your combined tax bracket—including the surcharge—would be only 17.25 percent. "It usually doesn't pay to buy tax-free investments in order to save only 17.25 percent in taxes," he says. "You'll usually make out better investing in taxable investments.'' (A taxable bond paying 9 percent provides 29 percent more than a muni paying 7 percent.)

3 IF YOU WOULD BENEFIT, CONSIDER MORE THAN JUST MUNICIPALS.

Taxpayers who might be smart to invest in additional tax-favored investments to get a double-barreled blessing, says Feiertag, are those in the 28 percent bracket who haven't reached the limit on their surcharge—which translates into about $5,300 in taxes for single taxpayers and $10,700 for couples where both are eligible.

Such investors need not consider only tax-free municipals—such as those offered through no-load mutual funds, like Vanguard in Valley Forge, Pennsylvania, which is famous for its low expenses.

They might also move more of their assets into tax-deferred Series EE savings bonds and into growth stocks, which don't pay much in the way of dividends.

Watz also suggests variable annuities, which can be invested into a variety of mutual funds, including money-market funds. Such annuities let investors accumulate earnings tax deferred, and after the annuitant dies the money escapes the costs and delays of probate.

Gau mentions all-cash real estate limited partnerships, the income from which may be partly or entirely sheltered by depreciation deductions. He also suggests investing in low-income housing partnerships, which provide special tax credits, though he warns that such investments can be risky.

The accountant also recommends ''split'' annuities, where you invest one sum into a ''deferred'' annuity, and another sum into an annuity that immediately starts showering you with payments. You won't owe taxes on the earnings from the first annuity until you start withdrawals. The immediate annuity gives you your original investment back, so most of the payments you receive over time aren't taxable. Using two annuities, you can arrange it so that, after a few years, you wind up with the same amount of money you started with, despite your withdrawals.

Have an insurance broker make the arrangements, using two different insurance companies, Gau advises. If you use just one, the IRS may give you trouble.

For more information about the Medicare Catastrophic Coverage Act of 1988, phone the IRS at 1-800-888-1998.

4 DON'T WORRY ABOUT UNDERESTIMATED ESTIMATED TAX PAYMENTS DUE TO THE SURCHARGE.

You get a break. While you should figure out what the extra charge will be, any underestimation of your tax bill—due to the surcharge—that you make during the first year you're subject to the surcharge will not expose you to a penalty.

Medicare (Part A) Surcharges and Maximums

Tax Year	Extra Rate Per $150 of Tax Liability	Maximum ($)	Percent of Income Tax
1989	22.50	800	15
1990	37.50	850	25
1991	39.00	900	26
1992	41.50	950	27
1993	42.00	1,050	28

WILL TAX-EXEMPTS HELP YOU?

Here's what you must receive from a tax-free investment to equal the return on an investment subject to Federal taxes as well as the Medicare surcharge. (State income taxes aren't figured in because they vary. If only one spouse is eligible for Medicare, the 32.2 percent rate ends at $33,480.)

Taxable Income	Combined Tax Rate (percent)	6%	7%	8%	9%
		Equals a Taxable Yield of			
Single $0 to $18,850 Joint $0 to $30,950	17.25	7.25	8.46	9.67	10.88
Single $18,850 to $27,720 Joint $30,950 to $52,400	32.20	8.85	10.32	11.80	13.27
Single $27,720 to $44,900 Joint $52,400 to $74,850	28	8.33	9.72	11.11	12.50
Single $44,900 to $104,330* Joint $74,850 to $177,720*	33	8.95	10.44	11.94	13.43
Single $104,330* Joint $177,720*	28	8.33	9.72	11.11	12.50

*Figures should be increased by $11,200 for each personal exemption above one for single, above two for joint.

Chapter Two
EVERYONE'S 1040

To remind you of some recent changes:

• you no longer get extra exemptions for being blind or sixty-five or over—you get a higher standard deduction instead

• if you can be claimed as a dependent on someone else's return, such as your parents', you can't claim an exemption for yourself

• you cannot get a dependency exemption for children twenty-four years old or older, even if they are full-time students, if they have an income of more than $2,000, whether earned or unearned. But if the child provides more than 50 percent of his or her own support, the child can take the personal exemption

• you must provide a Social Security number for any dependent two years old or older by the end of the year

• you must separate your dependents into the number of children who lived with you, the number who didn't live with you (because of divorce or separation), the number of your parents, and the number of your other dependents.

This chapter will provide tax-saving suggestions, beginning with the whole process of filing your return and proceeding through listing your exemptions. The next chapter will pick up with reporting your income, and carry you through the amount you owe—or, let us fervently hope, the amount of your refund.

AVOIDING AN AUDIT

5 **SALES PEOPLE, WATCH OUT.**

The tax returns of people in certain occupations are more likely to be audited. If you're any of the following, be especially careful in preparing your return—and especially scrupulous about keeping good records: beauticians, cab drivers, direct-sales people, independent contractors, real-estate settlement lawyers, salespeople, stockbrokers, waiters, and waitresses. People in these occupations enjoy this unusual attention, obviously, because of the opportunity they have to conceal some of their income.

6 **EXPLAIN ANYTHING UNUSUAL.**

If you had (say) $25,000 in unreimbursed medical bills last year, attach a letter giving the names of the physicians, hospitals, and other health-care providers you consulted, along with their fees.

If you received a check on January 1, 1990, and the payer gave you a Form W-2 showing you received the money in 1989, don't declare it in 1989—but append a note explaining the situation and promising to declare the income in 1990. The note should show that the amount reported on Form W-2, less the amount received in 1990, equals the amount reported on 1989 Form 1040.

By providing such explanations, you will raise the odds against your getting in trouble. Just clip your statement to the appropriate page, and on the IRS form write, "See attachment." On any such attachments, write your name, Social Security number, "Form 1040," and the tax year.

7 BE SPECIFIC.

Don't write something vague, like "public relations," under the miscellaneous deductions on Schedule A, for example. Specify the amounts spent for advertising, entertainment, and so forth.

8 AVOID FREQUENT AUDITS.

If you've been audited on a particular item within the past two years and received a "no change" report, you might be safe this time. Tell the IRS that you should be exempt, under its "repetitive audit plan."

FILING

9 DON'T GIVE THE IRS A RUBBER CHECK.

The penalties have increased—from 1 percent of the amount due to 2 percent. If what you owe is less than $750, the penalty may be only $15, though. If you have a good excuse you can get off the hook.

10 HAVE THE IRS FIGURE OUT YOUR TAXES.

Benefit: If you think you'll owe taxes, you may get a grace period. You must file Form 1040A or 1040EZ by April 15. The IRS, of course, will need time to figure out what you owe. And once it tells you, you'll have thirty days to pay up, without being charged any interest.

The rules for having the IRS figure out your taxes: Your income must consist only of wages, salaries, tips, interest, dividends, pensions, and annuity payments; your adjusted gross income (your total income minus things like deductible contributions to pension plans) must be $50,000 or less; you must take the standard deduction and not itemize your deductions; and you must file your return by April 15.

11 GET PERMISSION TO FILE LATE.

You could be hit with a penalty if you don't submit your return on time. But there's a simple solution: You can obtain an automatic four-month extension to submit Form 1040 (or the easier 1040A) just by filing Form 4868 by April 15. But you must have paid all your taxes by April 15. Submit what you estimate you owe with Form 4868.

You can get still more time to file your return only if you have a good reason. File Form 2688. Submit it early to give the IRS time to consider your request. Good reasons: Your tax records were destroyed by fire; your tax preparer died or is ill; third parties (your employer, a bank, an investment adviser) failed to provide you with information you need to complete your return.

12 DON'T FILE A "FRIVOLOUS" RETURN.

You may get socked with an immediate $500 penalty if you submit a return that's clearly incorrect, or doesn't have sufficient information. Example: A taxpayer had two dependents and claimed ninety-nine exemptions.

13 FILE A RETURN JUST TO GET A REFUND.

Even if you don't have to file a return (because you didn't have sufficient income, depending on your filing status), submit a return for a refund. This might be the case if you worked part-time and taxes were withheld from your paycheck. Or if you are entitled to the earned-income credit. (See Chapter 3.)

FILING STATUS

14 FILE A JOINT RETURN EVEN IF YOUR SPOUSE DIED.

Usually, you will pay less taxes if you file jointly rather than singly. And if your spouse died on January 1, you can still file a joint return for the rest of the year. By the same token . . .

15 FILE A JOINT RETURN IF YOUR SPOUSE DIED WITHIN THE PAST TWO YEARS.

You can benefit from the lower tax rates of filing jointly for two years following your spouse's death, provided

• you could have filed a joint return with your spouse during the year of the spouse's death, even if you didn't;
• you have not remarried; and
• you have furnished over half the cost of maintaining a home that was the main residence of a dependent son, stepson, daughter, or stepdaughter.

Once two years have elapsed, you can claim head-of-household status. (See Tip 18.)

16 CONSIDER FILING SEPARATELY FROM YOUR SPOUSE . . .

if the two of you earn about the same amount of money, and if one of you had very high medical expenses . . . or large, uninsured casualty losses . . . or high employee business expenses . . . or if one of you is subject to the alternative minimum tax.

17 THINK HARD BEFORE FILING SEPARATELY.

The case against filing separately: The tax rates for separate filers are higher than for joint filers. If your spouse itemizes, you must itemize; if your spouse takes the standard deduction, you must, too—even if the standard deduction would be less than the total of your itemized deductions.

Besides, if you and your spouse are sixty-five or over, or you are both blind, you cannot get the extra per-spouse standard deduction if you file separately and you itemize—unless your spouse had no gross income and is not a dependent of another taxpayer.

If an elderly couple file separately, part of their Social Security income is taxed, whatever their income level. And by filing separately they cannot use the maximum of $25,000 of rental real-estate losses to offset regular income—only half the regular amounts are allowed. Such couples who file also lose the child-care credit and the earned income credit.

18 CONSIDER FILING AS A HEAD OF HOUSEHOLD.

You'll sometimes pay less in taxes than you would if you filed singly. Your tax rate may be lower, your standard deduction higher, and—unlike single people—you may be able to use the earned-income credit. To qualify, you must

• be unmarried or legally separated under a divorce decree or a separate-maintenance agreement on the last day of the tax year;
• pay over half the cost of keeping up the main home of a parent, whom you can claim as a dependent (you needn't live with the parent);
• pay over half the cost of keeping your own home, which was the home for more than half the year of one of the following: (a) your unmarried child, grandchild, foster child, or stepchild (none need be your dependent); (b) any person listed below whom you *can* claim as a dependent: parent, grandparent, brother, sister, stepbrother, stepsister, stepmother, stepfather, mother-in-law, father-in-law, brother-in-law, sister-in-law, son-in-law, daughter-in-law, and (if related by blood, not marriage) an uncle, aunt, nephew, or niece. Exception: These people don't qualify if you claim them under a multiple-support agreement (where a group of people band together to provide the support). See Tip 44.

19 FILE AS A HEAD OF HOUSEHOLD IF YOU'RE MARRIED . . .

but living apart from your spouse. Rules: You must file a separate return; you must pay more than half the cost to keep up your home; your spouse didn't live with you at any time during the last six months of the year; and your home was the main residence of your child or stepchild for over six months of the year—and you can claim your child or stepchild as a dependent.

20 REMEMBER: YOU DON'T HAVE TO LIVE WITH YOUR PARENT.

You can be a head of household even if your parent lives apart from you, in a hotel, house, apartment, or hospital, if your parent qualifies as your dependent.

21 MAKE SURE YOUR PARENT QUALIFIES AS YOUR DEPENDENT.

You must contribute more than half your parent's support to claim your parent as a dependent—and your parent cannot have an income of more than $2,000 in 1989. If you give your father $5,000 to stay in an apartment, and he used $5,000 (mostly from his savings) for his own support, he is not your dependent, and you cannot qualify as the head of a household. Giving him $1 more than he spends on support would have turned the trick.

22 FILE FOR HEAD-OF-HOUSEHOLD STATUS EVEN IF YOUR PARENT DIED DURING THE YEAR . . .

or if a child, who made you eligible for head-of-household status, was born during the year. You qualify so long as you maintained the person's primary residence during the part of the year that he or she lived with you.

23 INCLUDE DOMESTIC HELP AS A COST OF HOUSEHOLD UPKEEP.

To figure out whether you provided half the cost of a household, also include property taxes, mortgage interest, rent, utility charges, repairs and maintenance, property insurance, and food.

PERSONAL EXEMPTIONS

24 CLAIM AS MANY EXEMPTIONS AS YOU CAN.

They're worth a deduction of $2,000 apiece in 1989. And they qualify as deductions from your taxable income— without those annoying floors of 2 percent of your adjusted gross income, 7.5 percent, or 10 percent (for, respectively, miscellaneous deductions, medical deductions, and casualty deductions). You're entitled to a personal exemption for yourself and your spouse; you're also entitled to a dependency exemption for someone you support, such as a child.

But high-income taxpayers are losing the personal exemption. For single taxpayers, the phaseout begins when their taxable income reaches $93,130. For married taxpayers, the benefits decline once income reaches $155,320. For heads of household, it's when income reaches $128,810.

These exemptions will be eliminated by means of the special 33 percent tax rate, which eats away at the value of the personal exemption once your income climbs above the levels mentioned above. More about this in the next chapter.

Keep in mind, too, that if you claim a child as a dependent, the child can no longer use the personal exemption on his or her own return.

25 DIVORCE IN DECEMBER, MARRY IN JANUARY.

If you divorce in December, you can file as a single person for the entire current year, which usually lowers your taxes if both spouses work. If you marry in January, you can file singly for the previous year. (No, I'm not suggesting that the *same* couple divorce, then remarry. The IRS would not look kindly upon that.)

Of course, let's not overlook romantic considerations from these calculations!

26 REMEMBER THE HIGHER STANDARD DEDUCTION FOR THE BLIND AND SIXTY-FIVE OR OLDER.

You no longer get extra exemptions if you're blind, or sixty-five or older. But now you're entitled to a higher standard deduction. A joint filer who is elderly or blind is entitled to an extra standard deduction of $600 ($1,200 if both spouses are elderly or blind, or one is elderly while the other is blind). A single person gets an extra $750 deduction for being elderly or blind—$1,500 if both.

27 CLAIM THE HIGHER DEDUCTION FOR BLINDNESS IF YOU CAN'T WEAR CONTACTS.

Even if your eyesight would improve if you wore special contacts, you will be considered blind if the contacts cause pain or injury, and you can wear them only briefly (and regular glasses wouldn't help). If you are totally blind, meaning you cannot tell light from darkness, attach a note to your return. If you are partially blind (your vision is no better than 20/200 in your better eye, even with corrective lenses), attach a note from a physician or optometrist declaring that you are medically blind.

DEPENDENTS

28 CLAIM A FRIEND AS A DEPENDENT.

You can, if

• during 1989 your friend's gross income was under $2,000;
• you furnished more than half your friend's support;
• your friend used your home as a primary residence;
• your friend lived in your household for the entire year (temporary absences, such as for vacations, don't count).

Similarly, you can claim as a dependent a member of the opposite sex who is living with you and whom you are supporting—providing that, in your state, such a common-law arrangement isn't illegal.

A person qualifies as your dependent if

a. you furnish more than half the person's support;

b. the person's total or gross income isn't $2,000 or more during 1989, unless he or she is under nineteen or, if over nineteen but less than twenty-four, is a full-time student;

c. if not a close relative, the person was a member of your household and lived with you for the entire year. (Close relatives, who don't have to live with you, include: child or legally adopted child, grandchild, great-grandchild; stepchild; brother, sister, half-brother, half-sister, stepbrother or stepsister; parent, grandparent, or other direct ancestor; stepfather or stepmother; a brother or sister of your father or mother; a son or daughter of your brother or sister; your father-in-law, mother-in-law, son-in-law, daughter-in-law, brother-in-law, or sister-in-law.)

d. The person must be a citizen of this country, or a resident of this country, Canada, or Mexico during the year—or an alien child adopted by and living with a U.S. citizen abroad.

e. The person does not file a joint return with a spouse— unless the couple file merely to receive a refund.

29 CLAIM A CHILD WHO DIED AS A DEPENDENT.

While you can't claim a stillborn child, you can claim a child that lived even briefly.

30 HAVE YOUR TWENTY-FOUR-YEAR-OLD COLLEGE KIDS BECOME SELF-SUPPORTING.

They must contribute more than 50 percent of their own support now, if their income is $2,000 or over, to get an exemption. Otherwise, even if they're full-time students, their parents cannot get the exemption.

31 HAVE A BABY IN DECEMBER, NOT JANUARY.

One accountant I know argues that, by having a baby at the very end of the year, you get a dependency exemption for the eleven preceding months. (Talk about planned parenthood!)

32 OBTAIN A SOCIAL SECURITY NUMBER FOR EACH DEPENDENT.

You must list the number on your return. You'll need one for any child who is at least two by the end of the tax year. Otherwise, there's a $5 penalty.

▪3 CLAIM AN ILLEGITIMATE CHILD.

▪4 TAKE A DEPENDENT WHOM YOU DIDN'T SUPPORT FOR THE ENTIRE YEAR.

If your dependent moves out during the year, you can still claim him or her as a dependent if you provided over half of the support for the entire year and the person is a close relative. The length of time doesn't matter; the amount you spend does.

▪5 INDICATE WHICH OF TWO PARENTS YOU SUPPORT.

Let's say that you contribute $6,500 to your parents' support. They spend an additional $12,000 on their own support. The IRS would hold that you gave each parent $3,250. That, plus half of $12,000, means that their individual support consisted of $9,250. And your contribution of $3,250 is *not* over half of $9,250.

But if you had indicated in a note that your $6,500 went to only one of your parents, and you had given checks only to that parent, your $6,500 would have been over half of the $9,250—and you could claim that one parent as a dependent.

▪6 BE WARY OF CONTRIBUTIONS THAT DON'T COUNT AS SUPPORT.

Support doesn't include your payments of income taxes, Social Security taxes, or life-insurance premiums—or the cost of sending children to overnight camp. It does include cash, food and lodging, maid service in the home, education, medical and dental care, recreation, transportation, and "similar necessities." Thus, if you pay for someone's expenses of driving a car—oil, gas, insurance—that counts as support. If you give someone a TV set for that person's exclusive recreational use, include its fair market value.

37 DON'T OVERLOOK WEDDING EXPENSES IN CALCULATING SUPPORT.

Wedding apparel and accessories, the wedding reception, and flowers for the wedding party, the church, and the reception count toward support. So do music lessons, dancing lessons, books and supplies, clothing, laundry, dry cleaning, telephone bills, summer day camp, baby-sitters, entertainment (like toys and movie tickets), vacations, and charitable contributions made on behalf of the potential dependent. Furniture, appliances, and cars may also count.

38 PERSUADE A POTENTIAL DEPENDENT TO EARN LESS.

Let's say that your father has earned $1,000 in 1990, working part-time. You've contributed $2,000 toward his support. Once he has over $2,000 of gross income, you will lose him as a dependent—both because his total income is too high, and because you haven't contributed over half his support. Suggest that he cut down on his work, in return for your increasing your support.

39 PERSUADE A POTENTIAL DEPENDENT TO SPEND LESS.

Let's say that you might claim your father as a dependent except that he uses much of his savings or income to support himself. Urge that he save more of his money, or he give more to your own children. If your father saves his money, or gives it away, it doesn't count as self-support. So you might more easily qualify as contributing over half of his support.

By the same token, persuade a potential dependent child who's working part-time to save or invest some of his or her money, too, so it will be easier for you to contribute over half of his or her support. But remember that a $2,000 dependency exemption is worth only $360 for someone in the 28 percent tax bracket.

40 USE THE FAIR RENTAL VALUE OF A ROOM, NOT YOUR ACTUAL COSTS.

If a potential dependent lives with you, calculate the cost of the lodgings as what a renter would pay—not your proportionate expenses. Take into consideration the use of furniture and appliances, the cost of heat, electricity, and water. You'll usually make out better that way, because the fair rental value should include a margin for profit as well as a reserve for future repairs and maintenance.

41 DON'T INCLUDE THE VALUE OF SCHOLARSHIPS AS SUPPORT . . .

if the child is a full-time student. Thus, if you contribute $4,000 to a child's support, and the child has only a $5,000 scholarship, you're considered to be contributing *all* of the support.

42 DON'T INCLUDE SOCIAL SECURITY IN A DEPENDENT'S GROSS INCOME.

The maximum total income that a dependent can have in 1989 is $2,000—unless the dependent is a child under nineteen or a full-time student under twenty-four. But if an adult receives Social Security payments, you needn't include it in figuring his or her gross income. Still, if the adult spends the money to support himself or herself, you'll have to take the amount into consideration in calculating whether you passed another test—that you provided more than half their support—to claim the dependency exemption.

If your potential dependent receives Medicare reimbursements (Part A) and reimbursements for physician care (Part B), you can exclude them in determining whether you provided more than half the person's support. But local-assistance payments are counted as support made by your potential dependent.

43 PERSUADE A POTENTIAL DEPENDENT TO GET TAX-FREE INCOME.

If your mother has $2,050 in income from corporate bonds, bank interest, or Treasuries, you cannot claim her as a dependent for 1990. But if part of her investment income came from municipal bonds, that interest wouldn't count toward the $2,000 barrier. So persuade your mother to invest in munis. Other nontaxable income that doesn't count toward the $2,000: life-insurance proceeds, gifts, and inheritances.

44 IF YOU RECEIVE HELP WITH SUPPORT, DECIDE WHO WILL BENEFIT MORE FROM THE EXEMPTION.

Let's say that your mother gives you money to support your child. You and she should decide who should claim the child as a dependent. If you're in a higher tax bracket, you might be better off claiming the exemption—but not in so high a bracket that you start losing personal exemptions.

If you would benefit more, make sure that your mother's contributions are given to you to use as you wish—not for the child. Otherwise, she should apply her contributions directly for the child's support, such as paying the child's medical bills.

If you're divorced or separated, work out such an arrangement with the other parent. Generally, the parent who has custody of the child can claim the child as a dependent. But if the other parent would benefit more, tax-wise (the other parent might be in the 28 percent bracket, while you're in the 15 percent), you can work out a deal. If you're the custodial parent, you can give the other parent a declaration (Form 8332) that you won't claim the child as a dependent, so the other parent can—by attaching the declaration to his or her return. (Note: A pre-1985 written agreement might have given the exemption to the parent who didn't have custody if that parent provided at least $600 for the child's support during the year.)

Still another situation: You, your brother, and your sister contribute equal amounts to a parent's support. None of you can claim the parent as a dependent—unless the three of you file a multiple-support agreement, allowing just one of you to claim the dependency exemption. What you might do: Alternate claiming your parent as a dependent year by year.

Any person who furnishes over 10 percent of the support can claim the exemption, if the others agree to it, as long as all of you provide over one half the support. You'll need Form 2120.

45 TAKE A MARRIED CHILD AS A DEPENDENT . . .

if you provide more than half the child's support, the child's income isn't over $2,000 (for 1989), and the child and her spouse don't file a joint return (except to obtain a refund). Because you're probably in a higher bracket than your child's spouse, you'll benefit more.

46 TAKE A FULL YEAR'S DEPENDENCY EXEMPTION FOR SOMEONE WHO DIED.

You can do this even if the person died in January of 1989.

Chapter Three
DEEPER INTO 1040

Among the major tax changes in recent years:

• You must pay a 5 percent surtax if your taxable income is above certain amounts—so that your highest Federal rate may be 33 percent.

This 5 percent extra tax goes into effect, if you're single, when your taxable income is between $44,900 and $104,330 (and you have one exemption). It goes into effect, if you're married and filing jointly, when your taxable income is between $74,850 and $177,720 (and you have two exemptions). It goes into effect, for heads of households, when your taxable income is between $64,200 and $140,010 (and you have one exemption).

• There's another surtax, one you may not be as familiar with. You begin losing any personal exemptions (a deduction of $2,000 apiece in 1989) when your income goes over the levels mentioned above.

This phaseout starts for joint returns, when your taxable income is $177,720; for single individuals, at $93,130; for heads of households, at $128,810; and for married couples filing separately, at $117,895.

This surtax is the lower of (a) $560 times the number of exemptions you've claimed, or (b) 5 percent of your taxable income, minus $155,320, on a joint return; minus $93,130, on a single return; minus $128,810 on a head-of-household return.

Here's how it works: For every $11,200 of taxable income you have above the thresholds mentioned above, you lose one personal exemption that you've deducted.

Example: You and your spouse file jointly, and have $210,000 in taxable income. You've already subtracted $4,000 from your gross income for two personal exemptions.

The tax on your first $30,950 of your income, at 15 percent, is $4,642.50. The tax on the balance of your income, $179,050, at 28 percent, is $50,134. ($210,000 − $30,950 = $179,050.) Total tax so far: $54,776.50.

Next, you must pay a 5 percent surtax on the income you have between $74,850 and $155,320. The amount is $80,470. Multiply that by 0.05, to get $4,023.50. Total tax so far: $58,800.

The purpose of this 5 percent surtax is to eliminate the benefit of your having paid only 15 percent tax on the first $30,950 of your income. You paid $4,642.50. If you had paid 28 percent, the amount would have been $8,666. The amount you saved: $4,023.50. And that's what the 5 percent surtax has recaptured.

Now we come to surtax 2, the personal-exemption surtax. Your two personal exemptions amounted to $4,000. At 28 percent, you saved $1,120. Your joint income of $210,000 is $54,680 above the threshold of $155,320. Since you lose one exemption for every $11,200 of income above

$155,320, you lose both exemptions—for an extra tax of $1,120. Total tax: $59,920.

The purpose of surtax 2, the personal-exemption surtax, is to continue surtax 1, the extra 5 percent, not stop it at certain limits. In the example we've just given, you lost one personal exemption for every $11,200 of taxable income over $155,320. You had two exemptions; two times $11,200 is $22,400. You wound up paying $1,120 extra. And $1,120 is 5 percent of $22,400.

The tax table in the Appendix provides a much simpler way of calculating both surtaxes, and it uses different figures for taxable income. We've given a more complex explanation here, so you can understand the logic behind the whole thing.

To remind you of other significant changes that tax reform made: Now, you must report your tax-exempt income—from municipal bonds, for example. And you don't deduct $100 (or $200, if filing jointly) from your stock dividends. You don't pay taxes on just 40 percent of your long-term capital gains, but on 100 percent.

Moving expenses are no longer an adjustment to your income. You can deduct them (if you pass the usual tests) only if you itemize on Schedule A. That's where employee business expenses are now, too. And the deduction for a married couple who both work has vanished.

Gone, too, is the partial credit for political contributions.

INCOME

47 TRY AVOIDING THE 5 PERCENT SURTAX . . .

even if it means bringing income into 1989. If your taxable income will be taxed at 28 percent for 1989, but taxed at 33 percent for 1990, bring income into 1989.

Of course, if you think you may be in the 33 percent bracket this year, and not next, by all means defer income.

48 IN GENERAL, DEFER INCOME IF YOU CAN.

Despite the previous tip, if you're scheduled to receive any income late in the year, it's usually better to receive it early the next year instead. You'll have an entire year to spend or invest all that money without having to pay taxes—apart from whatever estimated taxes you might be required to fork over. The later in the current year you're owed the money, the better it would be to defer getting it. (If you could have received the money *early* in the year, you'll miss out on what the money could have earned for you during the first part of the year.)

Still another reason to postpone income: You may be in a lower tax bracket next year. Heaven forbid, but you may lose your job, or be disabled, or suffer a terrible business loss. That's less likely to happen *this* year, simply because this year is partly over.

Naturally, if you expect to be in a much *higher* tax bracket next year—because of raises or bonuses, or selling property or other assets—disregard the previous advice. Pull income into this year, not next.

To defer income, ask an employer to defer paying you for some work until early next year. But ask him or her *before* you perform the project, or the IRS will object. And get the agreement in writing, in case you don't trust your employer.

Self-employed? Postpone sending out bills for November and December until late in December or early in January.

49 DECLARE INCOME IN 1990 DESPITE FORM 1099.

Let's say you receive a check in early January 1990 for work you did in 1989. Your employer also sends you a 1099 indicating you were paid for 1989. Can you nonetheless declare the money on your 1990 return?

Yes, if there was no way you could have received the money earlier than January of 1990. Attach a statement to your return explaining that you didn't receive the income indicated on Form 1099 until 1990, and that you will declare it on your 1990 return. Keep the envelope, with its postmark, in which you received the money.

50 DOUBLE-CHECK YOUR W-2 FORM.

If you find an error on the W-2 form that your employer sends you, notify your employer and the IRS. The IRS will send you Form 4852. Fill it out and file it with your return.

51 DON'T REPORT AMOUNTS FOR PERSONAL-INJURY DAMAGE.

Money you receive from a personal-injury lawsuit (your doctor operated on the wrong knee, a neighbor made malicious remarks about you) aren't taxable. But in a recent case, a fifty-seven-year-old man tried to exclude the award he won in an age-discrimination suit. No go. The award was just compensatory damages.

52 DON'T REPORT OTHER TAX-FREE INCOME.

Such as

• child-care assistance your employer pays for, whether by providing the care directly or by paying someone else. Maximums before the expense is included in your income: $5,000 a year, $2,500 for marrieds filing separately. The amount you exclude cannot exceed your earned income. (If your expenses are greater than what your employer provides, the excess still qualifies you for the child-care credit, subject to certain limits.) Your employer can deduct the cost—an incentive for employers to consider offering this fringe benefit.

• tuition payments your employer makes—providing that your income is not above a specified level and that it's not for postgraduate work leading to a degree. Excluded: $5,250 a year.

• the value of any health-insurance policy your employer pays for you.

• up to $50,000 worth of life insurance for you, providing that all employees get the same treatment; premium payments on whole-life insurance that your employer paid *if* the benefits are lost if you leave your job. (Term is plain insurance; whole life comes with a savings account.)

• gifts you receive, or money you inherit.

• life-insurance proceeds when you're the beneficiary.

• money you receive from a health-insurance company to pay your medical bills (you subtract the money from your medical deductions).

• scholarship and fellowship money you receive for tuition and other course-related expenses, like books, supplies, and equipment—if you're working toward a degree. Scholarship money for room, board, and incidentals is now taxable—unless (a) the grants were made on or before August 17, 1986, or (b) on or after August 17, 1986, if you received the proceeds before January 1, 1987, to pay expenses incurred before that date. But scholarship money a child receives for room, board, and incidentals doesn't count as support—and does count as earnings, thus raising the child's standard deduction.

- supper money your employer pays if you must work overtime, and if you must account to your employer for the amounts you spent.
- the expenses that a would-be employer pays for you to come for a job interview.
- unemployment insurance if you purchased the protection yourself (but not if your employer paid for it).
- prize money that you donate to charity.
- employee awards for length of service and job safety (up to $1,600 a year per employee, and up to $400 for a nonqualified awards plan), and traditional retirement gifts.
- the value of small gifts your employer may present you with, like a turkey at Thanksgiving, or the use of the photocopying machine, or having a secretary type something personal for you.
- free services your employer provides when it doesn't cost him or her anything extra (like free flights to airline employees, free phone service to telephone company workers).
- reasonable discounts (up to 20 percent) your employer gives you on goods or services.
- money your employer provides to cover the cost of having someone care for your child or other dependent, thus enabling you to work (the person providing the care cannot be a dependent of yours, or a child of yours under nineteen); if the care is outside your home, it must cover a child under thirteen, or a dependent or spouse who is incapacitated and spends at least eight hours a day in your house.
- money your employer provides for tuition for your taking courses related to your job—up to $5,250—so long as it isn't graduate study.
- the cost of meals that your employer provides, if the meals are supplied at your employer's place of business and for his or her convenience (so you can be called upon for help even while you're biting into a hamburger), or if you're

allowed only a short time to eat and there are no adequate facilities nearby.

• a place to live that your employer provides on the business premises for his or her convenience, if you're *required* to live there. But if you have a choice of free lodging on the premises or a rental allowance for living elsewhere, and you choose the former, the value of the lodging is taxable income.

• free parking your employer provides for you at or near the office, business use of a company car, and subscriptions to business magazines your employer provides.

• contributions that your employer makes to your government-approved retirement plan (like a 401[k] plan).

• Social Security taxes your employer pays for you if you're a domestic worker or an agricultural worker.

• strike payments if they're made to both union and nonunion workers, the payment varies in accordance with a person's needs, you needn't do anything in return for the payments, and at the time you're not getting unemployment compensation or other government help.

53 DISTINGUISH BETWEEN SCHOLARSHIPS AND TAXABLE INCOME.

A university paid the tuition of a professor's kids at another school, and he didn't report the value of the tuitions, considering them scholarships. No way. They were part of his employer's payments to him.

54 DON'T PAY TAXES ON SOMEONE ELSE'S INTEREST.

Let's say that you have a joint account with a child, brother, or parent. The financial institution will report all of the interest or dividends to the IRS under the account's Social Security number.

If it's your number, but you split the income with the other person, report all of the proceeds on Schedule B. Then, right below that, subtract the amount belonging to the other person, and identify it as a "nominee distribution." Also file Form 1099-Int and Form 1096 with the IRS, and send a copy of 1099-Int to the other person.

55 DON'T INCLUDE THE FULL COST OF A BOOBY PRIZE.

Let's say that you win, as a prize, a free meal at an expensive steak restaurant—and you're a vegetarian. So long as any prize has flaws, or strings attached, and you refuse to accept it, you needn't report its value as income. If you do accept it, just report its fair market value—what someone might actually pay for it. Check around to see if anyone might buy it from you, and at what price.

56 KEEP FROM HAVING TAXES WITHHELD IF YOU WON'T OWE ANY.

If you work only a short time for modest wages, you probably won't owe any taxes—though taxes may automatically be deducted from your salary. Give your employer Form W-4, certifying that you owed no Federal taxes last year and don't expect to owe any this year.

57 DON'T REPORT AS TIPS WHATEVER WAS A PURE GIFT.

You're a waitress in a restaurant. A patron comes in, doesn't sit down, tells you that you remind her of her long-lost daughter, and gives you $100. Then she leaves. That's not a tip—it's a pure gift.

58 REPORT FORGIVENESS OF CERTAIN DEBTS.

A casino let a compulsive gambler off the hook on some of his gambling debts, and he didn't declare it as income. A court ruled him wrong.

INTEREST YOU RECEIVE

59 DON'T REPORT INTEREST ON . . .

tax-exempt state and local bonds; an individual retirement account, Keogh plan, pension plan, or profit-sharing plan, so long as you didn't make any permanent withdrawals. (But remember: Beginning with 1987 returns filed in 1988, you must list your tax-exempt interest. If you have a lot, be prepared for the IRS to inquire how you obtained the money to buy those bonds.)

60 MAKE SURE YOUR TAX-EXEMPTS ARE REALLY TAX-EXEMPTS.

Beware of certain municipal or state "private activity" bonds, the interest from which is taxable as of September 1, 1986. Such bonds usually pay more than general-obligation bonds. And beware of even tax-exempt private-activity bonds—such as those to finance airports and sewage facilities—because their interest will be considered a tax-preference item, a concern if you are subject to the alternate minimum tax. (See Chapter 16.)

61 MAKE SURE THE PAYER HAS YOUR CORRECT SOCIAL SECURITY NUMBER . . .

or you'll face penalties, and the payer can withhold 20 percent of your interest in the future. Look carefully at the 1099-INT statement you receive.

62 DON'T LIST INTEREST UNTIL YOU RECEIVE IT.

Don't report the interest on a certificate of deposit if (a) it matures (becomes payable to you) next year, and (b) its maturity isn't over a year, and (c) interest isn't credited to your account and can't be withdrawn except at maturity. Example: You buy a one-year CD in February 1990, and you receive your investment plus interest in February 1991. Report the interest in 1991, not 1990. The same goes for Treasury bills that mature next year.

63 DON'T DECLARE INTEREST YOU DIDN'T RECEIVE.

Examples: interest a bank or other financial institution credited to you but that you didn't really get because the institution was insolvent. (Some state-insured banks still haven't paid interest they owe from years ago.)

Also, interest you supposedly received, according to a Form 1099-INT, may be incorrect. Let's say you bought a bond, and paid the seller for "accrued interest"—the interest he or she is owed between payment periods, all of which will automatically go to you. When you receive Form 1099-INT, report the total interest on your return, and subtract what's known as the "purchased interest."

If you're receiving interest from insurance proceeds from

a life-insurance policy on your late spouse, who died on or before October 22, 1986, you can exclude $1,000 a year. This remains true even if you remarry.

64 HESITATE BEFORE USING YOUR CHILD'S SAVINGS FOR THE CHILD.

If you've given money to a child under a law like the Uniform Gift to Minors Act, don't use any of the income to support the child, else it will be taxed to you. In some states, you have a legal obligation to pay for your child's college education if you can afford it, so be careful about invading your child's assets even for that reason.

65 REMEMBER THAT INTEREST FROM SERIES EE SAVINGS BONDS MAY BE TAX-EXEMPT . . .

if the bonds were issued on or after January 1, 1990, and you use the proceeds of the bonds to pay eligible educational expenses. See the Introduction.

66 ROLL OVER YOUR SAVINGS BONDS.

You have a choice about reporting the interest on a Series E or EE government savings bond. You can report it year after year (few people do), or report the total interest when the bond is cashed in. And there's a third choice: When the bond is cashed in, you can make a tax-free exchange of the proceeds for another government bond (HH)—or just keep your bond beyond the maturity date, still collecting income. That will continue to postpone the date you must declare the interest you've accumulated.

Old Series E bonds have a final maturity of forty years

after they were issued. They are immediately taxable then and won't earn any more interest.

67 HAVE YOUR CHILD REPORT INTEREST ON SAVINGS BONDS IF . . .

the child is fourteen or older, and has very little income. The child's standard deduction may wipe out any tax due on the interest. If the child waits to report the interest, he or she may be in a higher tax bracket when the bonds are cashed in. (Much of the income of children *under* fourteen, remember, will now be taxed at their parents' highest rates.) The same strategy would hold for anyone who has very little income.

But keep in mind that you must *not* report the interest as it accrues if you plan to claim the new college-tuition tax credit.

DIVIDENDS

68 DON'T REPORT INSURANCE "DIVIDENDS" AS DIVIDENDS.

They're a return of premiums you paid that were more than the insurance company needed. As for the "dividends" you received from credit unions and savings and loan associations, they're really interest, and should be reported as such. Distributions made by money-market mutual funds are really interest on short-term obligations, but you do report them as dividends.

What *are* dividends? They're the money you receive because of your ownership of a corporation's stock. As mentioned, once upon a time, $100 ($200 if you filed jointly) was untaxed. No more. Still, dividends are nice to have—and not just because they're worth more now that tax rates are going down. They also provide some protection against a stock's going down too far and too fast. Generally, a stock paying a 5 percent dividend won't plummet as much as a similar stock paying a 3 percent dividend—because the more a stock goes down, the higher its yield (the dividend in conjunction with the stock's price) becomes, and the more attractive it is to investors interested in high income. (Of course, there's a danger that a company in really bad shape will reduce or eliminate its dividend.)

69 NOT ALL DIVIDENDS ARE TAXABLE.

A "return of capital" isn't taxable. What this means is that you're just getting back part or all of what you invested. And if a dividend is really just a return of your investment, it's not taxable. Your Form 1099-DIV should indicate as much.

But keep in mind that a nontaxable dividend lowers the basis (the purchase price, for tax purposes) of your investment. If you invest $100 in a stock, get $40 back as a return of capital, then sell the stock at $60, you don't have a $40 capital loss. You've broken even.

"Liquidating" dividends are also nontaxable. They're issued by companies going out of business, and at least part of what you receive will be just a nontaxable return of your investment.

Another instance where dividends aren't taxable: when you receive stock or the right to buy stock as dividends. The rules: You cannot choose to receive cash instead; and the stock isn't preferred stock—which pays higher dividends and has first claim over "common" stock if a company goes bankrupt.

TAX REFUNDS

70 DON'T REPORT STATE AND LOCAL TAX REFUNDS . . .

if you didn't itemize (list all your deductions on Schedule A). Reason: You didn't deduct for those taxes, so you've already paid your full Federal tax on those refunds.

If you paid the alternate minimum tax in a previous year, you might not have to report a state or local tax refund, either: In calculating the alternate minimum tax, you weren't allowed to take deductions for state or local taxes.

ALIMONY RECEIVED

71 DON'T REPORT ALIMONY UNLESS . . .

your ex-spouse can deduct the payments on his or her return. The ex-spouse cannot deduct them if they aren't made in cash, or if you and your ex live in the same household. Another rule: If annual payments exceed $15,000, they must not be "front-loaded" (most of the payments made in the early years). See Chapter 14 for more on alimony.

72 DON'T CONFUSE CHILD SUPPORT WITH ALIMONY.

If you receive child support, you are not required to report it as income, and your ex-spouse cannot deduct it. (Still, your ex-spouse might be able to claim an exemption for the child.) Property settlements are also not considered taxable alimony.

(For capital gains and losses, see Chapter 8; for pension income, see Chapter 15.)

SOCIAL SECURITY

73 CONSIDER NOT MARRYING.

If you and another person are receiving Social Security benefits, and have been planning to marry, you might think again—depending on your sense of morality. You might be better off, tax-wise, by not marrying. Perhaps this isn't so amoral as one might think; at your age, sudden illness could prove financially devastating, so you must think especially hard about money matters.

The reason you should consider not marrying: a married couple filing jointly will begin paying taxes on part of their Social Security benefits if their combined income is $32,000 or more. But two single people can each have incomes of $25,000 before their benefits are taxed—for a total of $50,000.

An accountant I know would even counsel two married people with combined incomes over $32,000 to get divorced. It's probably better than another alternative: that, while married, they not live together and file separately. In that case, the benefits of each spouse also wouldn't be taxed until they reached $25,000 apiece.

74 CHOOSE TAX-DEFERRED INVESTMENTS.

If you don't need the extra income immediately, consider buying growth (small company) stocks, those that pay low dividends or none at all; or buy Series EE savings bonds, and skip paying taxes on the interest until they mature or you cash them in. These tactics will also lower the threat that your Social Security income will be taxed, and may reduce the Medicare surcharge.

75 CONSIDER AVOIDING MUNICIPAL BONDS IF YOU ARE IN THE 15 PERCENT BRACKET.

Corporate bonds pay more, so think twice before investing in munis. Besides, when you calculate how much of your Social Security benefits are subject to taxes, muni bond interest is equated with ordinary income.

76 ALTERNATE GOOD YEARS AND LEAN YEARS.

Just as other taxpayers should consider bunching their deductions into alternate years, someone at risk of paying taxes on Social Security benefits or the Medicare surcharge might bunch income into alternate years—so that, during one of those years, he or she avoids the full taxes. Sell stocks for gains in one year, for example; sell stocks for losses in another year. Buy Treasury bills and certificates of deposit with interest that's taxable the next year, when they mature.

77 CONSIDER RETIRING LATER.

In 1989, those who retire at ages sixty-five to sixty-nine can earn up to $8,880 without losing any Social Security benefits. Above those amounts, they lose $1 for every $2 they earn. But at age seventy, they can earn any amount at all without losing Social Security benefits.

OTHER INCOME

78 REMEMBER WHAT INCOME ISN'T TAXABLE.

Some taxpayers are *too* conscientious. Or they just don't know the rules. Examples of nontaxable income:

- the value of fruit and vegetables you grow and consume yourself.
- insurance payments (for your wrecked car, for instance).
- forgiveness of student loans because you worked for a specified time in certain professions for certain employers (for instance, a young doctor's loan might be forgiven if he or she worked for two years in a rural area).
- debts you owed that were canceled as the result of a gift. Example: You owe a parent $500; he or she tells you to forget it. But if the debt was canceled because the lender simply despaired of ever collecting, you must report the forgiven balance as income.

Other income that you normally needn't report: life-insurance proceeds (unless the insurance was an "endowment" policy, which simply paid you for your investment—not for life insurance); health-insurance payments (unless you received a flat amount per day, not direct coverage of your expenses); Veterans Administration benefits; cost-of-living allowances if you work for the government; public-assistance payments; payments under a workers' compensation policy; insurance payment for the loss of a limb; insurance payment for additional living expenses because your residence was destroyed; stipends someone receives from a parent or spouse (yes, a child doesn't have to report a $5-a-week allowance); rebates that auto makers and others give to customers (they're really just reductions in the sales price); and, as mentioned, personal-injury awards (like money you receive from a successful libel suit, or for surrendering custody of a minor child).

79 DON'T INCLUDE PROPERTY EXCHANGES AS BARTER INCOME.

Barter exchanges must be reported by both participants. Example: You paint someone's house, he or she gives you legal advice, and no money changes hands. He or she must report the value of having his or her house painted; you must report the value of the legal advice. If you belong to a bartering club, and members exchange their services, you should receive Form 1099-B.

But an exchange of property isn't bartering. Bartering calls for the exchange of personal services.

Let's say that you trade your big old car to someone for her small new car; no money changes hands. So long as you clearly haven't made a profit on the deal, you needn't report any income. What if you trade a house for someone else's house, and the other house was worth far more than your house's basis (your total investment)? You may be able to postpone paying taxes on the gain. (See Chapter 11.)

Other income you *should* report: all unemployment compensation (as a result of tax reform); jury pay (but not a mileage allowance for commuting to the courthouse; and if you gave your jury pay to your employer, because he or she paid you your regular salary, you can take a deduction as an adjustment to income); partnership and S corporation income; royalties; hobby income; gambling winnings, though you can deduct your losses on Schedule A, up to your winnings (keep a record of all your losses, lest you win big at the end of a losing year); ill-gotten gains, as from embezzling, kickbacks, and something that the IRS calls "push money," or bootlegging.

ADJUSTMENTS

80 ADJUSTMENTS MAY BE WORTH MORE THAN DEDUCTIONS.

Actually, adjustments *are* deductions—but gold-plated ones. The differences between them and itemized deductions are:

a. Adjustments reduce your gross or total income directly. Deductions may be subtracted later on, after your gross income has been reduced by adjustments, and becomes "adjusted gross income."

b. You can always subtract adjustments from your income. But you can subtract deductions only if you itemize—and itemizing is becoming more and more difficult because the standard deduction is climbing. (See Chapter 4.)

Obviously, one reason adjustments are better is that you can always use them, whereas you can use deductions only when you itemize. The other reason adjustments are better: The bigger your adjustments, the lower your adjusted gross income. And the lower your adjusted gross income, the easier it will be for you to climb over the floor to deduct medical expenses (7.5 percent of your adjusted gross income), the floor for casualty and theft losses ($100 per occurrence and 10 percent of your adjusted gross income), the floor for miscellaneous deductions (2 percent of your adjusted gross income).

Alas, there aren't many adjustments left. Moving expenses have just moved over to Schedule A, as an itemized deduction, though without the floor of 2 percent of your adjusted gross income. And *un*reimbursed employee business expenses have also turned into an itemized deduction, *with* a floor of 2 percent of adjusted gross income.

What's left?

• Penalties you pay when you withdraw a time-deposit account early (for example, you put money into a certificate of deposit for a year, pull out the money after six months, and the bank hits you with a penalty).

• 25 percent of the health-insurance premiums you pay if you're self-employed (the remainder can be claimed as an itemized deduction, subject to the 7.5 percent floor).

• Alimony you pay. (Give your ex-spouse's name and Social Security number.) See Chapter 14.

• Finally, deductible contributions to IRAs, to a Keogh retirement plan for the self-employed, and to a Simplified Employee Plan for the self-employed. It's here that you can beef up your adjustments. Give as much as you can afford to your tax-deductible pension plans! And that advice applies to salary-reduction plans (like 401[k] plans) as well, because they provide the equivalent of adjustments to your total income, too. (See Chapter 15.)

CREDITS

81 REMEMBER: CREDITS ARE WORTH MORE THAN ADJUSTMENTS OR DEDUCTIONS.

A dollar's credit is worth a dollar of taxes saved. But adjustments and deductions don't reduce your taxes dollar for dollar—only up to 33 cents in 1989. Whereas credits are subtracted from the taxes you might owe otherwise, adjustments and deductions are subtracted from your taxable *income*. The meaning of all this: Nail down your credits!

Credits that ordinary taxpayers should pay special attention to: for child- and dependent-care expenses; for the elderly or for the permanently and totally disabled; and the earned-income credit, which is listed under PAYMENTS on Form 1040. Others: for foreign taxes, and a general business credit.

82 DON'T OVERLOOK THE CHILD-CARE CREDIT.

You are entitled to the child- and dependent-care credit if you provide more than half the cost of maintaining a household that includes at least one individual who qualifies you for the credit—and if you have dependent-care expenses related to your employment that you must pay in order to keep your job.

The credit can be up to $720 if you have one qualifying person in your household, $1,440 if you have more than one. But your adjusted gross income cannot exceed $10,000 for you to get these maximum amounts.

The qualifying individuals must be one of the following:

a. a person under thirteen whom you can claim as a dependent, or whom you *could* claim if he or she didn't have $2,000 or more of income;

b. a dependent who cannot care for himself or herself (you *must* actually claim this dependent, unlike the case above);

c. your spouse, if he or she cannot care for himself or herself.

How much can you claim? If your adjusted gross income is $10,000 or less, your credit is 30 percent of up to $2,400 of dependent-care expenses—if you have one qualifying person in your household. If you have two or more qualifying individuals in your household, your credit is 30 percent of up to $4,800.

For every $2,000 that your adjusted gross income climbs over $10,000, the 30 percent drops 1 percentage point. So, if your adjusted gross income is $28,000 or more, you can claim only 20 percent of up to $2,400 or $4,800—a maximum of $480 or $960. But no matter how high your income, you're entitled to 20 percent of the base expense amount—up to $480 for one child, $960 for two or more.

Here's how the percentages work out:

Adjusted gross income over . . .	Credit Percentage
$10,000	29%
12,000	28%
14,000	27%
16,000	26%
18,000	25%
20,000	24%
22,000	23%
24,000	22%
26,000	21%
28,000	20%

Dependent-care expenses include:

a. household services, such as for a housekeeper, cook, or maid, but not for gardeners or chauffeurs—and not, the IRS notes, for bartenders.

b. out-of-household services, such as the cost of a day-care center or a similar arrangement. A day-care center must have state or local approval; your dependent must spend at least eight hours in your household—he or she cannot spend almost all day at the center.

Important rules:

• Educational expenses don't qualify if the child is in the first grade or higher; only nursery or kindergarten schools are eligible.

• Any expenses count toward your credit only if they enable you to keep a money-making job, or look for one, or attend school full-time. If you do volunteer work for little or no pay, forget it.

• Your expenses can't be more than your income from your job if you're not married at the end of the year—otherwise, why work? If you *are* married at the end of the year, your expenses must be *less* than the earned income of you or your spouse, whichever is lower.

• If you (or your spouse) are a full-time student, or disabled, you are considered to have $200 of earned income for every month you're not working because of studying or disability—if there's one qualifying person. The income is $400 a month if there are two qualifying people. The disabled person can be the spouse. Why the $200/$400 arrangement? So you can deduct more of the dependent-care expenses.

• You can take the credit for expenses to pay only certain relatives to keep house for you, or take care of your dependents or your spouse. To qualify, these relatives cannot be claimed as dependents by either you or your spouse. (If they could, there would be lots of room for abuse—older brothers would be "paid" for taking care of younger brothers.) The relatives who qualify: a son or daughter nineteen or over at the end of the year; stepson or stepdaughter; brother, sister, stepbrother, stepsister; father, mother, or an ancestor of either (grandparents, typically); stepfather or stepmother; a son or daughter of your brother or sister; a brother or sister of your father or mother; a son-in-law, daughter-in-law, father-in-law, mother-in-law, brother-in-law, or sister-in-law.

• If you're married and living apart, you can claim the credit on a separate return only if (a) you maintain a household, (b) furnish half the cost for the year, (c) it's the main home of your child or other qualifying person for more than half the year, and (d) your spouse is absent for the last six months of the year. If you're divorced or legally separated, only the parent with custody of the child can get the credit. If you're married and living together, you can get the credit only if you file a joint return.

83 HIRE A PARENT TO CARE FOR YOUR CHILDREN . . .

if your parent isn't a dependent. This way, you can claim the child-care credit (if you meet the other rules), give your parent some extra money, and provide your child with loving care.

84 CLAIM CREDIT FOR PAYING A BABY-SITTER'S SOCIAL SECURITY.

In one case a parent who worked successfully deducted the payments she paid for her baby-sitter's Social Security. But she didn't get away with deducting the airfare to send her kids to stay with their grandparents during school vacations. No one, after all, was caring for the kids while they were flying.

85 CLAIM THE CREDIT EVEN IF YOU WORK ONLY PART-TIME.

But remember that your employment-related expenses cannot exceed your earned income.

86 CLAIM THE CREDIT EVEN IF YOU'RE OUT OF WORK . . .

providing that you're actively looking for a job.

87 DON'T SPLIT UP THE EXPENSES AMONG YOUR CHILDREN.

Let's say you have a housekeeper who watches your kids when they're home, but cleans your apartment while your twelve-year-old and your sixteen-year-old are in school. Use the full cost of housekeeper; don't apportion the expense between your eligible and ineligible children.

88 TAKE MEDICAL EXPENSES AS A CREDIT.

If there's any amount that's beyond the maximum, use it as a medical expense—if you itemize, if you can climb above the floor of 7.5 percent of your adjusted gross income. Don't try taking the expenses as a medical deduction, then use the 7.5 percent you can't deduct as a child- or dependent-care credit. It's not permitted.

By the way, not all of a child's medical expenses qualify for the child-care credit, such as routine medical or dental checkups.

89 DON'T OVERLOOK THE CREDIT FOR THE ELDERLY.

It can be worth $1,125 against your tax if you and your spouse are sixty-five or older. Overall, you may be entitled to a credit equal to 15 percent of the first $5,000 of your annual income. (Use Schedule R to figure out the credit.)

Even if you're under sixty-five, but you retired on permanent and total disability and your disability benefits are not tax-exempt, you may be entitled to this credit. You must have a physician complete the statement on the bottom of page 1 on Schedule R, attesting to the extent of your disability.

The flat amount you may be entitled to is reduced by

a. the nontaxable portion of your Social Security benefits, plus other tax-free retirement benefits; and

b. your adjusted gross income, or earned income beyond $7,500 for an individual, $10,000 for a married couple filing jointly, $5,000 for marrieds filing separately.

You won't be entitled to any credit if

• you're single, a head of household, or a qualifying widow or widower, and you receive nontaxable Social Security or other nontaxable benefits of $5,000 or more, or have an adjusted gross income of $17,500 or more.

• you're married, filing jointly, and only one of you is qualified for the credit—and together you have nontaxable benefits of $5,000 or more, or an adjusted gross income of $20,000 or more.

• you're married, filing jointly, and both of you are qualified for the credit—and together you have nontaxable benefits of $7,500 or more, or an adjusted gross income of $25,000 or more.

90 DON'T OVERLOOK THE EARNED-INCOME CREDIT.

This credit is available to low-income workers with a child claimed as a dependent. To be eligible, you must maintain a household for yourself and the child; the child must earn less than the dependency exemption ($2,000 in 1989), unless the child is under nineteen or a full-time student under twenty-four; and if you're married, you must file a joint return.

For 1989 the credit is 14 percent of your earned income up to $6,500—for a total of $910. This is reduced by 10 percent of your adjusted gross income or earned income, whichever is more, above $10,240. It's completely phased out at $19,340. You don't need a special form to claim the credit, but the IRS mails out a worksheet.

91 FILE FOR THE EARNED-INCOME CREDIT EVEN IF YOUR TAX IS ZERO.

You'll *still* get the entire amount of the credit. (Yes, there *is* negative income tax.)

92 GET THE CREDIT IN ADVANCE.

If you're sure you qualify, have your employer pay you the credit in your regular wages, by reducing any taxes withheld. Get a copy of Form W-5.

PAYMENTS

93 DON'T BE OVERWITHHELD.

Taxpayers who boast about the size of their refunds are actually revealing how little they know about taxes. They're proud of the fact that they lent Uncle Sam money at no interest whatsoever. You could have invested that money, or used it to pay other debts. Estimate what you'll owe for any tax year, and try to pay at least 90 percent of your estimate—certainly not over 100 percent. You can have your accounting department increase the number of your allowances for withholding.

94 DON'T BE UNDERWITHHELD.

You're subject to penalties if your tax payments don't total at least 90 percent of the tax you owe—or the full amount of the tax you paid last year—providing that the total tax you owe is over $500.

If you think your next year's taxable income will be the same as last year's, or higher, make sure you pay at least the amount you paid last year—either by means of withholding or through your paying estimated taxes. (With your withholding, claim one less allowance for every $2,000 in income you expect to owe taxes on.) If your income fluctuates, adjust your regular estimated-tax payments to keep up with what you think you'll owe.

But it's usually easier to pay 100 percent of what you paid last year than to estimate what you'll owe this year and pay 90 percent.

95 CATCH UP AT THE LAST MINUTE.

If you discover in November or December that you will be underwithheld, you still have time to increase your withholding. File a new W-4 form to bring your withholding to within 90 percent of what you'll expect you'll owe. You can reduce your allowances; you can file at the higher single rate, even if you're married; you can even have a specified amount regularly taken out of your salary. You can have as much withheld from your pay as you want—even to the point where you receive a paycheck for no money.

What if you don't have a salaried job? Have your spouse increase his or her withholding; or pay estimated taxes.

96 DON'T OVERPAY YOUR SOCIAL SECURITY TAXES.

You might—if you had two or more employers, and both withheld Social Security (FICA) taxes. The most you should pay for 1989: $3,604.80 on an income of up to $48,000. Either take the excess as a credit on your tax return, or—if one of your employers mistakenly withheld more than

$3,604.80—have your employer make up the difference in your next paycheck.

If you're self-employed, you will pay 13.02 percent on the first $48,000 of your net earnings from self-employment. The most you should pay for 1989 is $6,249.60.

It's possible to apparently earn less than the cutoff and still have too much Social Security taxes withheld. That could happen if you had two jobs, both of which provided salary-reduction plans. So, even if your W-2 forms indicated that you earned less than the $48,000 cutoff, you may have paid too much. Reason: Social Security taxes are deducted even from the portion of your two salaries that you salted away into 401(k) plans.

REFUND/AMOUNT YOU OWE

97 IF YOU OWE LESS THAN $1, FORGET IT.

But even if you're sure you'll owe less than $1, you must file a return if you meet the income thresholds.

98 SIGN YOUR RETURN.

If you don't, the IRS will ask you to resubmit a complete return. And if (a) you filed close to the deadline, (b) your completed return arrives after April 15, and (c) you owe a tax, you may be assessed a penalty for filing your return late. And your return is more likely to be audited.

99 IF YOU OWE MONEY, SEND EVERYTHING BY CERTIFIED MAIL.

Recently a couple told the IRS that they had sent their form in on time, but that it must have been lost in the mail. Then

they submitted a copy of their return—unsigned. The IRS
hit them with a late-filing penalty. And the tax court upheld
the IRS, ruling that the return wasn't filed because the
couple hadn't signed it—and that by not using certified or
registered mail, they had assumed the risk of nondelivery.
Until this decision, the IRS had discouraged taxpayers from
using registered or certified mail.

MISTAKES

100 MAYBE YOU WON'T OWE A PENALTY IF . . .

an officer or employee of the IRS gave you *written* erroneous
advice after January 1, 1989, in response to your specific
request. In fact, you may not even have any additional tax
to pay!

FOR HELP

101 ASK FOR HELP THROUGH PRP.

If you're entwined in red tape with Uncle Sam, try the IRS's
Problem Resolution Program. Check the phone book for the
local number. But before the PRP can help, you must have
made at least two attempts to clear up the problem by calling
the phone number listed on any letter you received from the
IRS.

Chapter Four
ITEMIZING

The IRS isn't eager for you to list all your deductions on Schedule A. That means more work for the IRS. To tempt you not to itemize, the tax folks give you an alternative: taking a fixed amount, the "standard deduction," instead. And to further tempt you, the IRA is raising the standard deduction.

	Standard Deduction—1989
Filing Status	
Married, filing jointly and qualifying widows/widowers	$5,200
Married, filing separately	$2,600
Heads of households	$4,550
Singles	$3,100

There's another advantage to taking the standard deduction. You're less likely to get into trouble with Uncle Sam. Taking the standard deduction means that the IRS won't question any write-offs you might have taken for medical expenses, for casualty losses, for a home office, and so forth—because you won't have claimed them.

This chapter will cover itemizing in general, taxes you've paid, interest you've paid, and miscellaneous deductions. As for medical expenses, casualty deductions, and charitable contributions, we'll cover those in the next three chapters.

And despite the IRS, we suggest that you

102 TRY TO ITEMIZE.

If you think that your itemized deductions will amount to more than your standard deduction, itemize. You have the money coming to you. Make a rough calculation of your deductions. Do they exceed the standard deduction for someone in your filing status? If they do, but only by $5 or some other tiny amount, you might stop there. But if it's a few hundred dollars, consider going for it.

There's a wonderful, little-known benefit of itemizing, besides any extra money you can collect: You'll become more familiar with the tax rules about deductions. And that knowledge can help you save money year after year.

Under certain circumstances, you *must* itemize. For example, if you're married, file a return separately from your spouse, and your spouse itemizes on his or her return.

103 DON'T SUBTRACT THE STANDARD DEDUCTION FROM YOUR ITEMIZED DEDUCTIONS.

A natural mistake. Before 1987, you would deduct the "zero-bracket amount" from your allowable deductions.

Reason: The tax tables had been adjusted to include the zero-bracket amount. But the new tax tables don't have the standard deduction built in.

Subtract your itemized deductions directly from your adjusted gross income. Take the number of personal exemptions you're entitled to, worth $2,000 for 1989. Then consult the tax tables to see how much money you owe—or how much Uncle Sam may owe you.

TAXES YOU PAY

104 DON'T THROW AWAY YOUR SALES-TAX RECEIPTS.

True, sales taxes are no longer deductible. But they add to the "basis" (cost, for tax purposes) of whatever you buy. If an item you purchase (an antique, a Mercedes, a painting) grows in value and you sell it, you can subtract the sales tax you paid from your taxable profit.

105 PERSUADE YOUR MORTGAGE HOLDER TO PAY YOUR PROPERTY TAXES EARLY.

If you think you can itemize this year, and the bank that collects your mortgage also pays your property taxes, ask to have the payments scheduled for January paid in December. A tax deduction in the hand is usually better than one in the bush. But if you definitely cannot itemize and thus deduct your real-estate taxes for the current year, forget it. If you pay your real-estate taxes directly, not through a bank, it will be easier for you to pay your property taxes either this year or next.

106 DEDUCT STATE ESTIMATED-TAX PAYMENTS FOR NEXT JANUARY . . .

if you actually make the payment this December, and you think you can itemize this year. (The day you mail or deliver your check is generally the date of payment.) Of course, you have nothing to gain by making your January Federal estimated-tax payments in December.

107 DEDUCT PERSONAL PROPERTY TAXES.

Example: the fee your state may require you to pay for a license for your car, based upon the car's value.

108 DEDUCT ON YOUR FEDERAL RETURN ANY ADDITIONAL STATE AND LOCAL TAXES . . .

that you may be assessed from a prior year's return as the result of an audit or an amended return. The extra tax, and 20 percent of any interest on it, is deductible.

109 DEDUCT FOREIGN INCOME TAXES . . .

or take them as a credit—see which way yields a lower tax. In any case, you can't deduct taxes allocable to wages you have excluded, using the foreign earned-income exclusion.

110 DEDUCT ANY STATE DISABILITY TAX WITHHELD FROM YOUR PAYCHECK.

List it under "Other State Taxes." Your contributions as an employee to state disability funds in California, New Jersey,

New York, or Rhode Island, as well as to the Alabama and
New Jersey unemployment compensation fund and the
Washington State supplemental workers' compensation fund,
qualify. Examine your salary check, and add up your total
yearly contributions.

111 FILE A JOINT RETURN WITH YOUR SPOUSE . . .

if you pay the real-estate taxes, but your spouse owns the
house. If you file separate returns, you will lose the deduction on your return.

112 DON'T DECLARE A RENT REBATE.

Let's say that you're a tenant, your landlord receives a tax
rebate, and he or she generously passes along part of it to
you. Don't include it as income. As a tenant, you usually
haven't been able to deduct your rent, so a tax rebate isn't
a return of any deduction you took. By the same token, you
need not report a state or local tax refund if you didn't
itemize in the year the refund was for.

113 DEDUCT YOUR SHARE OF THE TAXES . . .

if you own a cooperative apartment. Tax reform has given
cooperatives more flexibility in how they apportion real
estate taxes and interest among tenant-shareholders.

114 DEDUCT MORE THAN TAXES ON JUST YOUR CONDO.

You also pay your share of the taxes on elevators, corridors,
swimming pools, and other "common" areas. Make sure

that these taxes are added to the taxes you pay for your individual unit.

115 DEDUCT LOCAL TAXES FOR MAINTENANCE AND REPAIR OF STREETS.

If the taxes were for improvements (widening, lengthening), though, all you can do is add the taxes to the basis (cost, for tax purposes) of your property. This may lower your taxable gains when you sell your residence.

116 DEDUCT STATE AND LOCAL TAXES ON FEDERALLY EXEMPT INTEREST.

If (say) you live in California, and own a (say) South Carolina municipal bond, Uncle Sam won't tax you on the interest from that bond. But California will. Don't make the mistake of thinking that if California does, you can't deduct the California tax on your Federal return.

117 CHECK TAXES WITHHELD FROM YOUR FOREIGN INVESTMENTS.

If your stockbroker is holding the securities for you, he or she may not be informing you that foreign taxes have been withheld from payments to you. If that's the case, consider adding the extra interest or dividend income to your income, and taking a tax credit—which may be worth more than the additional tax you'll pay on the extra interest. (File Form 1116—"Computation of Foreign Tax Paid.")

118 DON'T PAY REAL ESTATE TAXES FOR A RELATIVE.

If you pay property taxes on a child's home or a parent's home, you cannot deduct the cost—because you're not obligated to make the payments. And they, of course, cannot deduct the cost because they didn't pay it.

INTEREST YOU PAID

119 PAY INTEREST THIS YEAR RATHER THAN NEXT.

The amount of "consumer" interest you can deduct is dropping. In 1987, it was 65 percent. In 1988, it was 40 percent. In 1989, it's 20 percent. In 1990, it may be 10 percent, or it may shrink to zero. Consumer interest is interest on credit cards, auto loans (even if you, as an employee, use the car for business), student loans, and such—not mortgage interest, not investment interest, not business interest. So, if you owe money on a credit card or have other consumer debts, try to pay them off in 1989 rather than 1990.

120 REDUCE YOUR CONSUMER DEBT.

If you use credit cards, discipline yourself to pay your bills on time, so as not to incur interest charges. These charges are now unconscionably high. Watch out for cards that hit you with interest if you have any charges at all, or if you're a few days late in paying one month's debt, and your next month's debt (which you haven't even been billed for) is over a certain amount.

If you use credit cards and cannot help owing interest,

choose a card that charges the lowest interest rates around. A credit-union card is usually a good bet. Or use a charge card, like American Express, which normally doesn't assess interest but expects you to pay your debts promptly. Or consider a home-equity loan, because the interest you'll owe may be fully tax-deductible. (See Chapter 11.)

121 PREPAY JANUARY'S MORTGAGE IN DECEMBER . . .

if you think you can itemize this year, but you're not sure about next year. (Remember: Mortgage debt is generally deductible in full, unlike consumer debt; so, unlike consumer interest, there's no reason to speed up payments.) If your lender's yearly notice reports that you've paid one month's less interest than you're claiming on your tax return, just attach an explanation to your return—"January mortgage interest paid in December."

122 DON'T BE AFRAID OF BORROWING.

In general, borrowing is less desirable now, with interest deductions being curtailed. But let's say that you have $5,000 to invest in a certificate of deposit; if you invest $10,000, you might receive a significantly higher return. So, you may be better off borrowing $5,000 (this interest is generally deductible in full, up to your investment income) to get the higher rate on a $10,000 investment. Work out the figures, using the different rates available and considering your tax bracket.

123 REDUCE YOUR INVESTMENT INTEREST.

Tax reform has lowered the amount of interest that you can deduct if you borrow money to invest. By 1991, you will be allowed to deduct such interest only to the extent of your net investment income—your investment income minus investment expenses (but not minus investment interest).

In the meantime, you can still deduct part of your excess investment interest. If you're married and filing jointly, the amount you use to calculate with is $10,000. Use $5,000 if you're married and filing separately.

For 1989, you can deduct 20 percent of excess investment interest, up to $10,000; for 1990, 10 percent; and in 1991, you cannot deduct any amount above your net investment income.

Your investment *income* doesn't include property used in your business. And your investment *interest* doesn't include any rental (or other "passive") activity income or loss, or any expense to obtain a stake in a passive activity. (See Chapter 10.)

Any disallowance can be carried forward to the next year. But in 1990 you'll still have to adhere to the shrinking amount of the deduction.

124 DON'T OVERLOOK ANY INTEREST EXPENSES.

You can toss into the pot

• "points" you pay when you obtain a mortgage to buy or improve a house. (Points, also called loan-origination fees, are special charges a lender socks you with to keep the interest rate down; each point equals 1 percent of the loan amount.) To be deductible all at once, you must *pay* the points all at once, not pay them as you pay off your mortgage; and you must pay them separately from other charges the lender assesses you with (ask for a separate bill, and pay by a separate check).

Other rules: Lenders must usually charge these points in your area, and the number of points you were charged should also be standard. Points paid, or supposedly paid, by owners when they sell a house to someone with a Veterans Administration-backed loan aren't deductible.

• points you pay to refinance your mortgage. Here, you can deduct the points only over the life of the mortgage. If you pay 3 points on a $100,000 loan, you wind up owing $3,000. If yours is a fifteen-year mortgage, you can deduct $200 a year. If, before the fifteen years are up, you pay off the mortgage—because you sell the house, or you refinance—you can deduct the remainder of the points in that year.

• certain penalties. Let's say that you *do* pay off your mortgage early. The lender may hit you with a charge of a few hundred dollars, especially if you clear up the mortgage in the first few years. This penalty, unlike most other penalties, can be deducted. Also, if your mortgage-holder assesses you an extra charge because you paid your monthly installment late, that late charge is fully deductible. So are penalties levied by credit-card and charge-card lenders, if the penalty is really extra interest, based on the unpaid balance, and not a fixed charge. The same goes for penalties for late payments assessed by an electric and gas company. But these are considered consumer interest—only partially deductible.

• interest you owe because you didn't pay all the taxes you should have. (This is considered consumer interest, even if the taxes you owed were from your business activities.)

• a portion of the interest you owe on the mortgage the cooperative owns if you're a member of the coop. Remember: Interest on a mortgage may be fully deductible.

125 DON'T BE AFRAID OF HAVING DEBTS ALONG WITH MUNIS.

The rule is that you cannot deduct interest if you use money you borrowed in order to buy tax-exempt securities, like municipal bonds, annuities, or cash-value life insurance. But that doesn't mean, for example, that you can never have a mortgage and munis at the same time. There must be a direct link between the debts and the tax-exempt instruments before you are forbidden to deduct interest payments.

One woman borrowed money to pay her taxes; she could deduct the interest, even though she owned municipal bonds. So could a man who borrowed money to start a business, deciding not to sell the municipals he owned. Another taxpayer borrowed money to buy a business; there was an unforeseen delay in the purchase. So he temporarily parked the money in municipal bonds—and a court approved his deducting the interest he had paid.

126 BORROW TO BUY TAX-EXEMPT INVESTMENTS . . .

and deduct the interest if the tax-exempts are only a tiny part of your portfolio. The IRS rule: The tax-exempts should constitute less than 2 percent of the average basis (cost for tax purposes) of your portfolio investments and business assets.

You can also fully deduct the interest you pay when you borrow from your insurance contracts—if the interest is $100 or less, if you have a financial emergency, or if your borrowing is related to your business.

127 BORROW FROM YOUR STOCKBROKER ...

if you're determined to buy securities with borrowed money. His or her charges will be considered investment interest. You cannot use the money for noninvestment purposes if you want the interest to be totally deductible. Keep in mind, though, that using your margin account to buy stocks, Treasury obligations, or anything else is very risky, even for professional investors.

128 PAY A DEBT BY BORROWING ONLY FROM SOMEONE ELSE.

If you owe (say) Chase Manhattan $10,000, don't borrow $12,000 from Chase to pay off your $10,000 debt. The interest you owed may not be considered deductible at all. Borrow the $12,000 from (say) Citibank—or from your rich uncle.

129 BORROW FROM YOUR FAMILY.

You can deduct the interest you pay if the loan was genuine—it wasn't really a gift, or you weren't charged a ridiculously low interest rate. Provide your family member (a minor child qualifies) with collateral; spell out the terms (amount due, interest rate, and payment schedule) in a note. The benefit, of course, is that your family member enjoys a high rate of interest—or you enjoy a low one. Warning: If the loan is for more than $10,000, the interest rate can't be less than a specified Federal rate.

A man I know borrowed from his young son's custodial account. The father had just purchased a car, and was paying a bank 13 percent interest on the loan. He borrowed

from his son, used the money to pay off the bank, and began
paying the child 13 percent interest—far more than the child
could have earned safely elsewhere. And the father had all
of the bank's printed vouchers to guide him in repaying the
loan over the next few years. While borrowing from a
custodial account is considered perilous, in this case everything was so aboveboard and sensible that the man's
accountant and his lawyer gave their approval.

A man's wife refused to tell him about her plans to
divorce him. She agreed to tell him if he lent her money.
He conceded; she told all; the interest she paid was deductible. The same was true in a case where a wife lent her
husband money to start a business.

130 DEDUCT A ONE-TIME FINANCE CHARGE . . .

for each advance your bank adds to your charge-card
balance. The fees that banks have charged for this service
have run from 1 percent to 2 percent of the advance.

131 DEDUCT "IMPUTED" INTEREST.

Let's say that you buy a home from someone for $100,000,
and the seller gives you a mortgage at a wonderfully low
interest rate—5 percent. Actually, the house is worth only
$90,000. The seller is really charging you $10,000 for that
5 percent interest rate. In situations like this, you can deduct
the "imputed" interest rate—what you're really paying.
(When you sell the house and figure out your capital gains,
you'll have to use a purchase price lower than that
$100,000.) You may need professional help to figure out
what you can deduct. Or consult IRS Publication 537,
"Installment Sales."

132 DEDUCT USURIOUS INTEREST.

The IRS doesn't care that you pay an exorbitant rate of interest, a rate that infringes state usury laws.

MISCELLANEOUS DEDUCTIONS

133 DON'T SUBTRACT 2 PERCENT FROM ALL MISCELLANEOUS DEDUCTIONS.

Moving expenses, for example, aren't subject to the new floor you must surpass to deduct the assorted expenses gathered under "miscellaneous" deductions. The new floor: 2 percent of your adjusted gross income (your total income minus things like pension contributions and alimony you pay).

Other itemized deductions that bypass the new 2 percent rule:

• gambling losses—up to your income from gambling (this was meant as a favor to the many people now playing state lotteries).

• deductions for mortgage interest and real-estate taxes on a cooperative you own.

• expenses of "short" sales (when you sell a stock short, you borrow the stock, then actually buy it and replace it later on, when—you hope—the price has gone down; you'll owe regular dividends to the person whose stock you borrowed and you may have to spring for capital gains as well, if the stock's price went up).

• the work expenses of a handicapped person relating to the impairment (typically, paying an attendant to help on the job, and the cost of special tools).

- estate taxes on income you received from someone who died. This is money earned by a decedent that went to you, not subject to income tax, but where the decedent's estate paid a Federal estate tax on that income.
- certain "claims of right" you paid. Example: You reported income in a prior year, but you had to pay back that income (the payer may have successfully sued you for it, or paid you by mistake).
- certain employment expenses paid by performing artists (see Chapter 12).
- a premium you paid to buy a bond. If you paid more for a bond than its face value, your extra expense is deductible—year by year, until the bond matures or until the year you sell it. (A bond may have been selling for $1,200 a unit, when its face value was $1,000—because it originally paid an unusually high rate of interest, and you were therefore eager to buy it.)

134 DEDUCT FOR HELP WITH THE IRS.

Fees you pay to a tax preparer to seek a ruling from the IRS, and fees you pay to the IRS in this circumstance, are miscellaneous deductions, not business deductions, the IRS recently ruled.

135 DON'T FORGET ANY MISCELLANEOUS DEDUCTIONS.

Among them (and all are subject to the 2 percent of adjusted-gross-income floor): most unreimbursed employee business expenses, such as for travel, meals, and entertainment (but reduce meal and entertainment costs by 20 percent first); the use of your second and additional home phones for business; education expenses (see Chapter 12); the cost of searching for a new job in the same field you're in now; work clothes that are required but you can't normally wear outside the office, along with safety equipment like goggles and hard hats; certain costs of an office at home (see Chapter 13); subscriptions to business and trade publications you need for your job; malpractice or errors and omissions insurance; medical examinations your employer requires; employment-agency and career-counseling fees; a college professor's research, lecturing, and writing expenses.

136 DON'T FORGET INVESTMENT EXPENSES.

Examples are fees charged by your investment adviser or manager, or by a trust administrator; subscriptions to investment publications like *Sylvia Porter's Active Retirement Letter* (you expect me to mention a competitor?), *The Wall Street Journal,* and this book.

Other deductions you might overlook: fees paid to a custodian of property you have that produces income; a rented office and staff needed to watch your investments; fees you pay a lawyer to collect money owed to you, and other such legal costs (like summonses and court fees); IRA custodial fees; investment travel and entertainment expenses (the latter must be reduced by 20 percent first).

137 DON'T OVERLOOK TAX-RELATED EXPENSES.

Examples: What you pay someone to prepare your tax returns, or to give you tax advice about your employment contract, your business, etc.; appraisals to determine the amount of a casualty loss, or whatever you're contributing to a charity.

138 DEDUCT EXPENSES IN CONNECTION WITH A HOBBY . . .

up to your income from that hobby.

139 DEDUCT FOR SCHOOL PARTIES . . .

if you're a teacher. Add in gifts to students, art materials, reading materials.

140 DEDUCT FOR A SAFE-DEPOSIT BOX . . .

if you keep taxable securities there.

141 ASK FOR AN EXPENSE ACCOUNT.

Today, if your employer doesn't pay you directly for your expenses, you can deduct only 80 percent of unreimbursed business meal and entertainment expenses—and only that much if you itemize and your miscellaneous expenses surpass a floor of 2 percent of your adjusted gross income.

So it's time to ask your boss to be reimbursed directly, via an expense account, and not to be expected to pay such expenses yourself, out of your salary.

142 DEDUCT SHIPPING A SAILBOAT AS A "PERSONAL EFFECT."

A man in Florida was transferred to South Carolina. He deducted $1,796 for the cost of shipping his sailboat. The IRS demurred, saying the sailboat wasn't a "personal effect." But the tax court okayed the deduction, holding that personal effects include any items "intimately associated with the taxpayer." The Florida man and his family had used their boat frequently.

143 DON'T OVERLOOK ANY SMALL TRAVEL EXPENSES . . .

such as the cost of dry cleaning and laundry, and phone calls home, as well as transportation, food, and lodgings.

Travel expenses are those you incur outside the metropolitan area where you work, and if you remain overnight.

144 DEDUCT FOR THE COST OF SITUATION-WANTED ADS.

Other job-hunting expenses you might overlook: phone calls to set up interviews, photocopying of documents (like articles you've written or presentations you've made), photographs that accompany your résumés, stamps and envelopes to mail out résumés, and transportation to potential employers and to employment agencies. Remember that even if you turn down a job offer, or if you're turned down, you can deduct the expenses, as long as you were looking for a job in your current field.

145 DEDUCT THE COST OF A REWARD . . .

if you lost a briefcase or other valuable business property, and you paid for an advertisement and the reward.

146 DEDUCT THE COST OF ATTENDING A STOCKHOLDERS' MEETING . . .

if you went for a specific purpose (to complain about the officers' high salaries, for example) and if your holdings in the stock are a significant part of your substantial portfolio, which is large. Deduct travel, meals (subtract 20 percent first), and lodging.

147 DEDUCT THE EXPENSE OF VISITING YOUR STOCKBROKER . . .

if you went there for consultation, not to watch the ticker tape. The same is true if you visit an investment adviser, an accountant, or a lawyer who advises you on taxes or estate planning.

148 DEDUCT YOUR SHARE OF OPERATING EXPENSES FOR AN INVESTMENT CLUB . . .

except for expenses linked with tax-exempt income.

149 DEDUCT INSURANCE YOU BOUGHT TO COVER LOST TAXABLE SECURITIES.

If you lost a security, you won't be issued a replacement until you post an indemnity bond—in case the person who found the security cashes it in. You can deduct the cost, subject to the 2 percent floor on miscellaneous deductions.

150 TRY TO ITEMIZE YOUR MOVING EXPENSES.

You will lose these expenses, which can be high, if you can't itemize. That's why it's important to keep track of all your expenses, and to try to itemize in the year you move, or incur expenses for moving.

Thus, if you move in 1990 and your employer isn't covering the cost, try to lower your adjusted gross income (by giving the maximum to pension plans, for example). By lowering your adjusted gross income, you're more likely to be able to claim deductions with floors you must surpass—medical expenses, casualty losses, and certain miscellaneous expenses. Also try to bolster your deductions (by, for example, accelerating contributions to a charity).

Reasonable moving expenses paid by an employee or by a self-employed person in connection with his or her job are deductible—if they meet certain complicated requirements. Claim the deduction on Form 3903.

Deductible moving expenses are either (a) direct or (b) indirect. The chief difference is that there's no limit on the deduction for direct moving expenses, while there are limits on the indirect ones.

Direct expenses include:

a. the cost of moving household goods and personal effects (including crating and packing) from your old to your new residence, plus

b. you and your family's transportation expenses (including meals and lodging) while traveling from the old to the new residence.

Indirect expenses include:

a. the cost of any round trips (including meals and lodging) you and members of your household took mainly to find a new residence—providing that you have already obtained a new job, or (if you're self-employed) you've made "substantial" arrangements to begin working at the new location;

b. the cost of meals and lodging for you and members of your family during the thirty consecutive days after you get your new job and while you're staying in temporary quarters (whether you're still looking for a new residence, or waiting to move in);

c. the cost of selling and buying a new residence, or terminating an old lease, including lawyers' fees, escrow fees, appraisal fees, real-estate agent's commissions, ''points'' (a special fee for a mortgage), and title-insurance costs. (If you can't itemize, in some cases these costs can be added to the basis—cost, for tax purposes—of your new residence, or subtracted from the sales price of your old residence. That way, you'll reduce the eventual capital gains if you sell your house in a taxable transaction.

You can deduct *direct* moving expenses only if

a. you move to a new main job that's at least thirty-five miles farther from your old residence than the old job was (subtract the distance in miles from your old residence to your old job, then subtract that number from the distance from your old residence to your new job, and hope that you get at least thirty-five); and

b. during the twelve months after you're at your new job, you're a full-time employee for at least thirty-nine weeks— or, if self-employed, you work full-time for at least seventy-eight weeks during the twenty-four months after you arrive at the new location. Exceptions to these thirty-nine-week and seventy-eight-week requirements are listed below.

You can deduct *indirect* moving expenses only if they meet the requirements listed above for *direct* moving expenses. The amounts you can deduct for *indirect* expenses are

a. no more than $1,500 for trips to find a new house before moving, and for temporary living expenses at your new job; and

b. no more than $3,000 for the expenses of selling, buying, or renting a residence, minus the amount you're allowed under **a.**

151 CONSIDER WAITING BEFORE SEEKING A NEW RESIDENCE.

To deduct your moving expenses, you have a year to move after you start a new job. So if you begin your job late in the year, you might wait until the next year before moving— if you think that the next year you'll be able to itemize, but this year you can't. You'll have to balance your possible deductions against the cost of a temporary residence, as well as the deprivation of possibly not having your family with you.

152 YOU CAN MOVE FARTHER AWAY FROM YOUR NEW JOB IF . . .

your new residence is much more convenient to your new place of work. For example, at your new residence you may have better public transportation, or you can drive on a highway to your office, not back roads.

153 YOU CAN CHANGE JOBS IN YOUR NEW AREA . . .

and still meet the thirty-nine-week test, so long as you remain in the same general area. And you can even take some time off during those twelve months after you start a new job, because the thirty-nine weeks don't have to be consecutive.

154 YOU CAN FAIL THE TIME TEST . . .

and still deduct moving expenses, if you're in the armed
forces and moved because you were permanently transferred, or you moved to the U.S.A. because you retired, or
you were laid off (for reasons other than "willful miscon-
duct"). The IRS generously adds: "The time test also does
not have to be met in the case of death."

155 DEDUCT MOVING EXPENSES EVEN IF YOU'VE NEVER WORKED BEFORE.

A student (for example) starting a first job can deduct
moving expenses, providing that the student moved from a
former main residence to a new one. (A college dorm isn't
a main residence.) The same goes for people entering the
job market after a long period of not working outside the
home—like a homemaker.

156 IF YOU HAVE A LOSS ON SELLING YOUR HOME . . .

you can't deduct it. So try to deduct a real-estate agent's
commission as a moving expense, not as an expense of
selling your home. What if you have a gain on your sale?
If you've also reached the $1,500 limit on house-hunting and
temporary living expenses, and the limit of $1,500 on home
sales expenses *without* the sales commission, use the
commission to reduce the gain on the sale of your house—
to lower your possible capital-gains taxes.

157 RENTERS CAN DEDUCT LEGAL FEES . . .

to extricate themselves from a lease; for payments to their landlords for freeing them from a lease; for a real-estate agent's fees; for the difference between the rent they pay now if it's higher than the rent they receive from the person to whom they sublet their residence; and for the cost of finding a replacement tenant. In renting a new residence, you can also deduct legal fees and the fees of a real-estate agent.

158 DEDUCT A LOST SECURITY DEPOSIT.

If you were renting and lost your security deposit because you broke your lease, it's deductible—but not if you lost the deposit because of damage to the residence.

159 DON'T CURTAIL HOUSE-HUNTING TRIPS.

There's no limit on the trips you can take, and still deduct the expense, once you have a new job.

160 DON'T DEDUCT JUST 9 CENTS A MILE IF YOU USE YOUR CAR.

You're probably better off keeping a record of your actual expenses for oil and gas, parking fees, and tolls.

161 DON'T GIVE UP IF YOU DIDN'T MOVE TO YOUR NEW AREA IN A YEAR.

If you had a good reason for your delay, you may be excused—and your moving expenses will remain deductible.

Example: You wanted your daughter to graduate from her old high school. (But, oddly enough, not having sold your old house yet isn't an acceptable excuse.)

162 DEDUCT FOR MOVING BACK TO THE U.S.A. . . .

if you retire while working or living overseas, or if you are the survivor (spouse or dependent) of someone who died while working overseas. (See Chapter 12 for other deductible expenses for employees.)

Chapter Five
MEDICAL EXPENSES

Tax reform made few changes with regard to your deducting medical expenses on Schedule A. But one of those changes was a beaut.

Now, if you itemize your deductions, the only medical and dental expenses you can actually write off are those that exceed 7.5 percent of your adjusted gross income (your total income minus things like deductible contributions to IRAs). The old percentage was 5 percent. This means that you must have very large, unreimbursed medical expenses before you can deduct anything. If your adjusted gross income is $30,000, you must have $2,250 in medical expenses before you can start deducting anything.

What can you do? Push or pull medical expenses into a year when you think (a) you'll be able to itemize, and (b) you'll have unusually large medical expenses. In other words,

163 BUNCH YOUR DEDUCTIONS.

One way is to pay your bills either this year, or next—assuming that your bills arrive near the end of the year. If you're strapped for cash, you can pay your bills by credit card this year, and take deductions this year, while paying the credit-card company next year. (If you would incur high credit-card interest, forget it. Just delay your payments.)

You can also postpone some of your sessions with health-care people. Perhaps a few of your possible expenditures are "elective"—you needn't have them done immediately. You can have your teeth capped this year or next. Or get bifocals this year or the following one. Or postpone a gallbladder operation if your doctor says, "It should come out one of these days." Or defer surgery that's just to improve your appearance. Needless to say, don't postpone any medical or dental care you really need, just to save on your taxes.

If you decide to try pushing health expenses into, say, 1990, also try to speed up expenses you would normally incur in 1991 into 1990. Get your physical early. See your dentist a little sooner. And pay your bills in 1990—even if your doctors or dentists haven't sent them (because they're practicing "bunching," too).

What if you expect to surpass the 7.5 percent floor in two consecutive years? Push your medical expenses into the year in which you may have a higher income—because you might be in a higher tax bracket, and deductions will save you more money.

If it's impossible for you to decide in which year your medical expenses may exceed 7.5 percent of your adjusted gross income, try to make your expenditures early in any current year. You'll have the remainder of the year to add to them. And it's almost always better to obtain deductions as soon as possible—so you'll have more income sooner.

164 DEFER FILING FOR HEALTH INSURANCE PAYMENTS.

There is another way to push your expenses into another year. Let's say that you have an appendectomy late in the year. You might file for reimbursement in December, knowing that you won't receive payment until January. When you receive your payment, you'll declare it as income in that year—instead of subtracting it from your medical expenses the previous year.

165 ASK FOR MORE HEALTH-INSURANCE COVERAGE.

Tell your employer you'll be satisfied with a smaller raise this year if your health-insurance coverage is more comprehensive, or there are lower deductibles, or you won't be charged anything for coverage.

166 REMEMBER THAT THERE'S NO TOP LIMIT ON MEDICAL EXPENSES.

While there's a floor (7.5 percent of your adjusted gross income), there's no ceiling. You can deduct all your medical-dental expenses to the point where you owe no taxes at all.

167 INCLUDE THE COST OF CHILDBIRTH CLASSES.

While this doesn't normally qualify, a woman who takes classes in order to play a more active role in her childbirth (that is, without complete anesthesia) can deduct the cost.

168 INCLUDE MORE THAN YOUR OWN EXPENSES.

You can include your own expenses and those of your spouse if you file a joint return, as well as bills you paid for

a. all dependents you list on your tax return;

b. any person (like a child or parent) you *could* have listed on your return as a dependent *if* that person didn't have at least $2,000 or more in income (for 1989), and didn't file a joint return with his or her spouse.

Example: You contributed more than half your mother's support, but you cannot claim her as a dependent because she had $2,000 in gross income during 1989. Yet you can include any of her medical expenses that you yourself paid as your own medical expenses.

Who else's expenses can you include? The surgical, hospital, laboratory, and transportation expenses of someone who came to your hospital to provide you with a body organ—for example, a kidney.

Another possibility: You can pay and deduct the medical expenses of a child you've made arrangements to adopt— even if the child isn't born yet! The child must have qualified as your dependent when the medical services were furnished, or when you actually paid them.

169 DEDUCT MEDICAL EXPENSES YOU PAID FOR A NONDEPENDENT CHILD . . .

if you were divorced under a decree after 1984. You can't deduct such medical expenses if you were divorced under an earlier agreement.

170 CONSIDER PAYING YOUR PARENTS' MEDICAL BILLS.

If they have relatively low taxes and relatively high medical bills, think about paying their medical expenses. If your payments of their medical bills, plus other support you give them, add up to over half their total support for the year, you may reap three tax advantages: (a) you can deduct the medical expenses you pay, (b) you may be able to claim them as dependents on your own tax return, and (c) if you're not married, you may be able to use the lower head-of-household tax rates in figuring what you owe.

171 DEDUCT THIS YEAR FOR LIFETIME CARE.

If you paid a lump sum for a dependent's or spouse's lifetime care in a retirement home, or the lifetime care of a handicapped child, you may be able to deduct the cost in the year you made the payment. But in general, for medical expenses to be deductible, you cannot pay them in advance.

172 INCLUDE THE COST OF PRESCRIPTION MEDICINES AND INSULIN.

Keep your receipts. Or consider patronizing a pharmacy that will send you a report on all your prescription purchases for the year; many pharmacies are happy to oblige.

You cannot deduct the cost of drugs unless prescribed by a physician. If your doctor tells you to take two aspirin and call him or her in the morning, deduct the doctor's bill as well as the cost of the phone call—but not the aspirin, which isn't a prescription drug.

173 INCLUDE THE COST OF INSURANCE YOU PAY FOR.

Not just health insurance ("basic" or "first dollar," as well as major medical), but dental insurance, "catastrophic" insurance (special policies that give you a maximum coverage of perhaps $1 million), and Medicare Part B. Also include the cost of belonging to a health-maintenance organization.

If your employer charges you for group coverage, your payments are deductible. Many employers don't inform their employees, at the end of the year, how much the employees have paid for health insurance. Either ask for an accounting, or keep your salary-stub checks and add up the totals.

Insurance you buy for accidental death, or loss of limbs, doesn't qualify. Nor does the cost of insurance that pays you a flat amount per week or month while you're ill or not working—because that insurance doesn't necessarily cover medical expenses. And skip the insurance you pay for the medical expenses of anyone injured in your car or by your car, or in your house.

Of course, any deductions you claim must first be reduced by reimbursements you received for medical-dental expenses. But you need not reduce your expenses by payments you've received for personal injuries, or for loss of your earnings, or the flat fees that a policy pays you if you're ill and out of work.

174 DON'T OVERLOOK ANY OTHER INSURANCE YOU PAY.

Does your child's school charge you for insurance in case your child is injured in sports? Does your child's summer camp? The premiums are deductible. So is the cost of insuring your contact lenses against loss or damage.

175 DEDUCT 25 PERCENT OF YOUR HEALTH-INSURANCE EXPENSES DIRECTLY FROM GROSS INCOME . . .

if (a) you're self-employed (the remaining 75 percent is an itemized deduction, subject to the 7.5 percent floor); (b) your health-insurance plan also covers your employees; (c) your deduction doesn't exceed your income from self-employment; and (d) you're *not* also employed by someone else, and don't have the option of joining your employer's plan, or the plan of your spouse's employer, at a reduced rate.

This special break is to give the self-employed a benefit like the one enjoyed by employees who receive health insurance free of charge.

But this concession applies only to tax returns for years after 1986 and *before* 1990. It might expire in 1990.

116 KEEP YOUR GAIN IF YOU HAD EXCESS INSURANCE COVERAGE.

Let's say that your hospital stay cost you $600, and two insurance policies paid you a total of $800. If you actually paid the premiums on the policies—your employer didn't pay either one—you need not declare or pay taxes on the gains you made. If some of your insurance was paid by you, some by your employer, you'll have to apportion your profit.

If you're reimbursed in the year after you had medical expenses, report the payments as income in the year you received them. But don't report more than any amount you previously deducted as a medical expense. If you didn't claim any deduction for those medical expenses—because you didn't itemize, or you didn't surpass the floor or you knew you wouldn't be reimbursed—again, you needn't report the reimbursement as income.

117 INCLUDE THE COST OF TRANSPORTATION.

Figure in the cost of cab fare, buses, trains, planes, or your driving to and from a doctor's office, hospital, pharmacy, or to a laboratory. You can either calculate the expense at 9 cents a mile, or total up the real costs (if you drive, your mileage plus what you pay for gas, plus any oil your car needs). Don't deduct for car depreciation, repairs, maintenance, or insurance. Whether you use the 9-cents-a-mile approach, or the actual cost, throw in whatever you paid for tolls and parking.

178 DEDUCT THE COST OF A TRAVELING NURSE . . .

if he or she accompanies you to a clinic, and gives you care you need (like medications or injections) during the trip.

179 CONSIDER DEDUCTING UNUSUAL TRAVEL COSTS.

A woman with a rare skin disease went to Europe to be treated by a doctor knowledgeable about her disease. She could deduct her travel costs along with his fees.

A man traveling to Europe on a freighter for a vacation had a recurrence of a severe kidney disorder. He flew back to San Francisco for emergency treatment by his urologist, and deducted the higher cost of the plane trip.

180 ADD THE COST OF HOTELS . . .

or other lodgings if you traveled somewhere mainly to be cared for by a physician in a licensed hospital or similar health-care facility. The cost of the lodgings can be for the patient and for another eligible person, like a parent accompanying a dependent child. Be careful not to claim the cost of a luxury motel, or spend time sightseeing or vacationing.

181 DEDUCT THE COST OF A TRIP TO A WARMER CLIMATE . . .

if a physician prescribes it to help a chronic ailment you (or your spouse or dependent) has, like asthma. But you can't deduct the cost of meals and lodgings on your visit unless you stay in a hospital. And you cannot deduct the cost of a trip to a weight-reduction spa, or for the improvement of your general physical or mental health.

182 DON'T FORGET A VARIETY OF OTHER EXPENSES.

Such as the cost of

- ambulance service
- phone calls to doctors, nurses, hospitals, insurers, and so forth
- artificial limbs, braces, elastic stockings, canes, crutches, wheelchairs, orthopedic shoes (beyond the cost of normal shoes), eyeglasses, medically needed whirlpools
- fluoridating devices recommended by a dentist
- contact lens solutions and supplies
- blood-sugar tests
- guide dogs (for the blind or deaf), along with their care and feeding, as well as other helpful animals
- books and magazines in Braille (above the cost of ordinary versions)
- special telephone equipment for the deaf, along with repairs
- hearing aids and their maintenance (including batteries)
- special instruction in speech and lip-reading for a deaf person
- special therapy for someone recovering from a stroke

- removal of lead-based paint from the walls of a house in which a child contracted lead poisoning from eating such paint. (Either the area must be within the child's reach, or the paint must be peeling or cracking, and thus likely to fall.)
- a special mattress and headboard if you have arthritis.

183 INCLUDE THE EXTRA COST OF CERTAIN ITEMS.

Examples:

- a TV set, or an adapter for an existing set, to provide subtitles for someone who's deaf;
- a car designed to accommodate a wheelchair, or special controls in a car for the handicapped.

184 BE IMAGINATIVE.

Here are other real cases, just to prompt you to consider other possible expenses:

An orthodontist recommended clarinet lessons for a boy with a severe malocclusion. The cost of the clarinet, along with the lessons, was deductible.

A woman who made her living donating blood was permitted to deduct the cost of high-protein food and vitamin supplements.

A woman worked as a clerk in her husband's store. Her mother needed home care, and the woman agreed to help her—on the condition that her brother pay another clerk to replace her in the store. The brother agreed, and deducted the store clerk's salary as a medical expense on his own return.

A man deducted the legal fees he paid to obtain guardianship over a relative who had refused psychiatric treatment.

A woman had to move to a larger apartment to accommodate a new nurse she needed, and deducted the extra rent she had to pay.

185 DEDUCT SOCIAL SECURITY TAXES . . .

you may have to pay on the wages of a nurse or attendant whom you hired directly.

186 DEDUCT THE COST OF COSMETIC WORK.

You can include the cost of hair transplants performed by a surgeon or a dermatologist, or a face-lift (even if a physician didn't recommend it), or having excess hair removed via electrolysis by a state-licensed technician.

A woman who had lost her hair as a result of a disease was allowed to deduct the cost of a wig that her doctor recommended to prevent her from becoming depressed.

187 DON'T DEDUCT THE COST OF HAVING YOUR EARS PIERCED.

Or getting tattooed.

188 WRITE OFF THE COST OF PRESCRIBED BIRTH-CONTROL DEVICES.

Examples: birth-control pills, a diaphragm, a vasectomy, female sterilization, an abortion.

189 DEDUCT THE COST OF AN AIR CONDITIONER WHEN YOU HAVE AN ALLERGY ...

if (a) your doctor prescribed it mainly to relieve your breathing, and gives you a statement saying so; and (b) the air conditioner is detachable—it isn't built into the wall of the house (that would turn it into an improvement that boosts the value of your house). Subtract from your deduction whatever salvage value you think the air conditioner may eventually have—what you might sell it for.

If you buy a vacuum cleaner to remove dust from your residence, to deduct the cost you would again need a physician's recommendation, as well as evidence that you wouldn't have bought it except for your allergy. (You might argue that you already had a carpet sweeper that did all the cleaning needed.)

190 DEDUCT THE COST OF A DRUG-TREATMENT CENTER.

Treatment at a center for alcoholics also qualifies.

191 DON'T DEDUCT THE COST OF A CENTER THAT HELPS PEOPLE STOP SMOKING.

Not, as Mr. Spock would say, logical, but it's the law.

192 DEDUCT THE COST OF A WEIGHT-REDUCTION PROGRAM ...

if a physician prescribed it *not* just because you're a little overweight, but because of a specific medical condition you

have—like a heart problem compounded by your excess
weight, or even for obesity (being grossly overweight).

193 WRITE OFF THE COST OF A SWIMMING POOL . . .

if it was recommended by your physician, and if you first
subtract the amount that such a permanent improvement
added to the value of your house. (If it's a removable above-
ground pool, subtract the salvage value.) Thus, if the pool
cost $20,000, and adds $5,000 to your house, your deduction is $15,000. (Swimming pools rarely add much to a
house's value unless you live in a state where the weather
tends to be warm year-round.)

To demonstrate that a pool was installed for health
reasons, you would be wise to buy a low-cost and not a
luxury model. And skip a diving board or slide.

One couple were able to deduct their pool by demon-
strating that they never entertained people there. But another
couple weren't allowed much of a deduction, even though a
doctor had recommended a pool for the wife's spinal condition. The pool was oversized, built with hand-cut stone and
cedar woodwork, in a building with a cathedral ceiling.

If your new pool is indoors, you can deduct a percentage
of your home-heating costs that warm the room it's in.

The same guidelines apply to most other medically related
home improvements—permanent air conditioners, central air-
conditioning, home elevators or inclinators, and bedrooms
and bathrooms added to a lower floor so that a patient
doesn't have to do much stair-climbing. (For exceptions, see
Tip 196.)

First subtract the amount that the improvements add to the
value of the house. (Many real-estate agents can do such
appraisals.) And don't buy the top-of-the-line model, or your

deduction may be limited to what a moderately priced improvement would have cost you.

194 DEDUCT FOR QUASI-HOSPITAL ROOMS.

A man rented a two-room apartment in his building for his mother, who, her physician had advised, needed extended care after being hospitalized. The son hired a full-time nurse, and furnished the rooms with medical equipment. He was allowed a full deduction for the rent because the rooms were similar to what a hospital or extended-care facility would have provided.

In a similar case, a man wasn't allowed to remain in his hospital room after an appendectomy. So, on his physician's advice, he checked into a nearby hotel until he recovered. His wife changed his bandages and helped him get around. The hotel's cost was deductible: It was regarded as a substitute for a hospital room.

195 DON'T FORGET OPERATING EXPENSES.

The electricity that runs the air conditioner for your allergy, and the cost of having it repaired and maintained, are deductible. The same goes for other doctor-recommended devices, like the cost of maintaining and running an elevator for a heart patient, or a special bath for an arthritis patient.

196 DON'T SUBTRACT THE VALUE OF CERTAIN IMPROVEMENTS.

Thanks to tax reform, you can now deduct the full cost (above the floor of 7.5 percent of your adjusted gross income) of removing structural barriers in a personal residence to make life easier for a handicapped person.

Thus, the following expenditures do *not* add to the value of a residence, for tax purposes: (a) constructing entrance or exit ramps; (b) widening doorways; (c) modifying interior doorways and hallways to accommodate wheelchairs; (d) installing railings and support bars in bathrooms, along with similar changes; (e) lowering kitchen cabinets and other equipment to make it easier for the handicapped to reach them; (f) adjustments of electrical outlets and fixtures.

197 DEDUCT THE COST OF AN OLD-AGE HOME FOR YOUR PARENT . . .

to the extent that your money goes for nursing or medical care. Ask the home to provide you with a breakdown of the charges. If your parent is in the home mainly for medical reasons, you can even deduct the cost of meals and lodgings.

198 DEDUCT THE COST OF A SPECIAL SCHOOL FOR A HANDICAPPED CHILD.

Examples: A blind child attends a school to learn Braille, a deaf child to learn lip-reading, a retarded child to receive special instruction. (While such a school may provide some normal educational classes, this cannot be the school's main purpose.)

Similarly, you can deduct the cost of remedial-reading courses if a child is brain-damaged, and the cost of a halfway house (including room and board) for a patient making a transition from a mental hospital to life in the community.

If your visits to and from the school are considered necessary for the child's therapy, your travel expenses may also be deductible.

199 DEDUCT PART OF THE COST OF HOUSEHOLD HELP FOR A SEMI-INVALID.

Divvy up the wages you paid between deductible medical care and nondeductible personal services, like house-cleaning. (One court let a couple deduct 75 percent of the expenses.)

200 HIRE YOUR RELATIVES.

You can have them care for an invalid, pay them, and deduct whatever percentage was purely medical. This is generally true even if your relatives have no medical or nursing training. If someone not licensed as a nurse provides nursing services, the cost may be deductible if those services were recommended by a physician.

If a relative, or a regular nurse, cares for someone in your home, deduct the cost of meals you provide, along with any wages you pay.

201 DON'T OVERLOOK THE FEES OF UNUSUAL THERAPISTS.

You can, of course, deduct fees paid to medical doctors and osteopathic physicians, dentists, optometrists, nurses, and psychologists. But you can also write off the fees of nonmedical doctors like

- acupuncturists
- chiropodists (podiatrists)

- chiropractors
- Christian Science practitioners
- unlicensed psychotherapists

Parents were allowed to deduct fees paid to a teacher trained to deal with dyslexic children. The reading disorder, in this case, was caused by brain damage; it might not have been deductible otherwise.

The experience, qualifications, and title of the therapist don't matter. What matters: that the services rendered are medically required.

In a case where an osteopath was treating a patient by manipulation, payments the patient also made to masseurs were deductible. And—are you ready for this?—payments by a Navajo Indian to tribal medical men for healing ceremonies were allowed.

202 DEDUCT THE COST OF CONTROVERSIAL MEDICATIONS . . .

if prescribed by a physician and purchased and used in an area where the sale and use are legal. Example: laetrile.

203 CONSIDER FILING SEPARATELY . . .

if you or your spouse had very high medical or dental bills. Figure it out both ways, separately and joint. Should one spouse have enormous bills, he or she may be able to surpass the floor of 7.5 percent of adjusted gross income— and reduce the total taxes you must pay.

Chapter Six
CASUALTY AND THEFT LOSSES

One important change that Tax Reform '86 made: You must file for insurance reimbursement (or estimate your insurance reimbursement) before you can take any deductions.

The amount of your casualty loss is the *lesser* of

a. the drop in the fair market value of your property, or
b. the cost of your investment in the property (your "basis").

Let's say that a burglar made off with your jewelry. It was worth $5,000; of course, it's valueless to you now. Loss: $5,000. But if you had paid only $4,000 for the jewelry a few years ago, $4,000 is your loss.

There are two reductions you must make before you can write off personal casualty losses:

1. subtract $100 from each separate occurrence (a fire and then a flood, for example), then

2. subtract 10 percent of your adjusted gross income (your total reportable income minus things like deductible IRA contributions) from your remaining casualty losses.

Business casualty losses aren't subject to these reductions.

Deduct insurance payments or other reimbursements you receive, or *may* receive, from the value of any loss. As mentioned, you're now required to file for insurance coverage before claiming casualty losses on your tax return—even if you're worried that reporting an accident to your insurance company may raise your premiums, or provoke the insurer to stop covering you.

Here's an example of how to calculate your deductible loss:

You bought a house for $25,000. (This is, presumably, *many* years ago.) Fifteen years later, it was worth $100,000. After a fire, it was worth only $50,000. An insurance company paid you $5,000 (unrealistic, but we need a low figure for our calculations). Your adjusted gross income is $32,500.

Value before fire: $100,000.

Value after fire: $50,000.

Decline in value: $50,000.

But remember that you're limited to the original cost of your house—$25,000. So forget about the $50,000.

If the insurance company had paid you $25,000 or more, our calculations would stop there. That's why we're using $5,000.

Subtract $5,000 from your $25,000 loss ($20,000); then subtract $100 ($19,900); then subtract 10 percent of your adjusted gross income (10 percent times $32,500 = $3,250), and you wind up with $16,650. This is your deductible loss—if you itemize, and if you have no other deductible losses that you can add to the kitty.

Our first piece of advice:

204 DON'T THINK OF JUST FIRES AND STORMS.

You may be also able to deduct losses for

- damage to your car
- theft or embezzlement
- cave-in damage on your property
- vandalism
- a burst hot-water boiler
- frozen water pipes
- earthquake damage
- damage inflicted by the pressure of ice
- damage to a business establishment (such as cracking of walls and ceilings) caused by shrinkage of subsoil in an unusually severe drought
- damage resulting from nearby blasting in a quarry
- damage to a septic tank caused by accidental plowing in the area

And let's not overlook losses from volcanic eruptions, shipwrecks, and sonic booms.

In general, you cannot take deductions for property you've lost or mislaid, for the drop in a house's value because of threatened future flooding, or for termite damage. To qualify, the losses you suffer must be the result of a *sudden, unexpected,* or *unusual* force.

A good example: A farmer was dynamiting some tree stumps on his property. His dog playfully retrieved a stick and deposited it under the farmer's car. The loss of the car was sudden, unexpected, and unusual.

Still other deductible losses: the value of honeybees destroyed by pesticide . . . the accidental poisoning of cattle . . . the death of a horse that had eaten the lining of a hat . . . replacing sand washed away from a private beach by an unusually severe storm . . . money you're swindled out of (if your state law considers it theft) . . . money to ransom someone who's been kidnapped.

In one memorable case, a wife left home; while she was gone, her husband gave some of her belongings to his girlfriend. The wife, a court ruled, was entitled to a theft-loss deduction.

205 DON'T APPLY THE REDUCTIONS TO BUSINESS LOSSES.

The $100 and 10 percent of adjusted-gross-income reductions don't hurt you if your loss was to business or income-producing property. Examples: fire damage to a room in your house you rent out, or use as an office; the theft from your factory of a photocopying machine. And with business items that are completely destroyed, or stolen, your deduction is your basis—even if your basis was *more* than the decline in the property's fair market value. (This is a special break businesspeople get.) But remember that your basis may have been reduced by depreciation, or by your taking the Section 179 expense election and writing off 10 percent of the cost during the first year. (See Chapter 13.)

206 DEDUCT LOSSES EVEN IF YOU'RE NOT THE OWNER.

If you're legally responsible for making good any loss, you can deduct it. Example: A tenant may be required to return rented premises to the condition in which they were originally—and thus be responsible for a fire loss. He or she can deduct the cost, subject to the usual reductions.

207 DON'T DEDUCT $100 FOR EACH DAMAGED ITEM.

If a fire destroys furniture, clothing, carpets, appliances, and books, the $100 reduction applies to all of them together, not separately. It's a $100 reduction per *casualty*.

208 DEDUCT WHICHEVER IS GREATER—THE COST OF REPAIRS OR THE DECLINE IN VALUE.

Your car cost you $8,000. A few years later, it was worth $5,000. After an accident, its value plummeted to $2,000. Obviously, you must choose the lower loss—not your basis, but the decline in the car's value, $3,000.

209 DON'T CLAIM THE VALUE OF CHEAP REPLACEMENTS.

If your Tiffany lamp was shattered by a windstorm, don't deduct the cost of a replacement you buy at a garage sale. Deduct the cost of the lamp, or its market value. By the same token, if you're replacing plants, bushes, or trees, deduct for the mature versions—not for the cheaper seeds or saplings you may have purchased.

210 DON'T BE QUICK TO ACCEPT AN INSURANCE SETTLEMENT.

A fire destroys your living-room furniture. You figure the loss at $5,000, but your insurance company, predictably, sets the loss at (say) only $3,000. If you accept the $3,000, you probably won't be able to deduct the remaining $2,000 as a casualty loss. The insurance company probably had you sign a paper acknowledging that the furniture's value was

$3,000. Unless $3,000 was the limit of your coverage, or you can come up with new evidence proving the furniture's value, you'll probably lose the remaining $2,000. Lesson: Give your insurer a hard time.

211 DEDUCT FOR LOSING MONEY IN A FINANCIAL INSTITUTION.

If you had money socked away in a nonbusiness account in a commercial bank, savings and loan, or credit union that went bankrupt or became insolvent, and you lost money, thanks to tax reform you can now take a casualty loss—instead of a bad-debt loss. (But not if you were an officer of the troubled bank, or owned 1 percent or more of the value of the institution's stock.) Claim the loss in the year when it became clear that you would never get your money back.

If you deduct such a loss as a nonbusiness bad debt, it's considered a short-term loss, and you must use it to offset capital gains—or deduct it from your ordinary income, up to $3,000 a year. You may be better off taking it as a casualty loss.

You can take a deduction for such casualty losses as far back as 1983, if you file amended returns.

212 DEDUCT CLEANUP EXPENSES, TOO.

Usually you can add these costs to your casualty loss—the cost of removing dead trees, for example.

213 DON'T FORGET THAT THERE ARE ALWAYS EXCEPTIONS.

A drop in the value of a house because of nearby flooding is *generally* not deductible. But in a case where a city decided to demolish nearby houses after a flood, a family was allowed a $12,000 loss for the decline in their home's value. The destruction of the other houses apparently was a key factor—their house had become something of an orphan.

214 DON'T DEDUCT FOR "MYSTERIOUS DISAPPEARANCES."

Mysterious disappearances of valuable property aren't usually deductible, but the loss of a diamond from a special ring setting was accepted after a jeweler testified that it must have happened as the result of a sharp blow.

215 DON'T DEDUCT FOR INSECT DAMAGE UNLESS . . .

the damage was done quickly. Pine beetles can wreak havoc quickly—and if they do their dirty work within around ten days, the IRS will accept such a casualty. Even termite damage has sometimes been held to be deductible. In one case, a builder and an architect testified that they had found no evidence of termites twelve months before they struck. In a similar case, the time period was fourteen months. (Such termites are sarcastically called "fast" termites.)

216 DON'T DEDUCT FOR ORDINARY DROUGHT DAMAGE.

Droughts tend to do damage gradually, and gradual losses usually don't qualify. But where trees died within a few months because of an unusual drought, the loss was permitted. A deduction was also allowed for damage to a home caused by a severe one-day smog. Damage to property caused by a freeze was permitted simply because it was unusual: It occurred in Florida.

217 DON'T CLAIM A DEDUCTION IF YOU'VE BEEN CARELESS.

Usually a person cannot claim a casualty loss if he or she was grossly careless—if he or she crashed a car while drunk, for example, or accidentally threw an envelope containing money into the fireplace. But when a husband slammed a car door on his wife's hand, smashing her ring, that was accepted as a casualty loss. Ditto the case of the husband who emptied a glass of ammonia down the garbage-disposal unit, unaware that his wife's diamond ring was rinsing in the glass.

Fire damage in a house was deductible, even though the fire department blamed the blaze on a careless cook. So was the loss of a lawn when the owner applied too much weed-killer. And the damage to a car resulting from the owner's having misjudged the space available in his garage. And damage to a car even though one man drove with bald tires, another with worn brake linings. Also deductible: A driver parked his car on an icy lake, and—well, you can guess.

But recall the general rule: You cannot be grossly careless and get away with deducting a casualty loss. Recently a man in Baltimore set some of his wife's clothes afire in his stove. He was a little annoyed at her—she wouldn't move to South Carolina with him, and apparently had been carrying on with another man. After setting her clothes on fire, he tried to quench the flames with pots of water. But the fire spread, and the entire house was destroyed.

The insurer refused to cover the damage. And when the man tried to deduct $97,900 as a casualty loss, the IRS balked. A tax court sided with the IRS: "We refuse to encourage couples to settle their disputes with fire."

218 DON'T FEEL BOUND BY A CAR'S "BLUE BOOK" VALUE.

The "Blue Books" are popular commercial guides to used-car prices. But if you can prove that your damaged car was worth more than the value listed, you can deduct a higher amount. Evidence: prices for similar cars being advertised for sale in your area.

219 DON'T INCLUDE EVERY BENEFIT AS A REIMBURSEMENT.

If your house burned down and a local agency provided you with free food, lodging, and clothing, you don't have to treat them as a form of reimbursement, and need not deduct them from your loss.

220 CALL THE COPS.

What's to prevent someone from hocking jewelry, then claiming it was stolen? Having to deal with the police may be one deterrent. That's why the IRS will be less skeptical if you've notified the police after you were the victim of a theft—and you've enclosed a copy of the police report with your tax return.

In fact, you're always wise to keep evidence supporting your casualty losses, such as newspaper reports about a storm, or bills showing what you paid for the painting needed after a flood. Photographs showing the extent of a casualty loss—after a storm, for example—will also bolster your case.

Yet sometimes you can deduct a theft loss even if you didn't notify the police. Examples: the disappearance of a diamond ring when the new cleaning woman disappeared directly thereafter. A teacher didn't report a break-in because, he explained, he suspected that students of his were the culprits. A man declined to prosecute a friend who had stolen something from him; his lawyer had concluded that court costs would be more than the value of the missing property.

If you've lost cash, how do you prove it? One man claimed that an envelope with $36,000 had been taken from his unlocked car. Fortunately, his secretary testified that she had seen him put $36,000 into an envelope to make a down payment on some real estate he was buying. A tax court believed them.

221 CHANGE THE YEAR WHEN YOU DEDUCT YOUR LOSS.

You can do this only in one case: You live in an area that the Federal government declares a disaster area. You can then deduct your loss either in the year the disaster occurred, or during the previous year by amending your return for that year. Amending your return might get you an immediate refund; then again, you might be better off waiting until next year if you're sure you can itemize then, or if your tax bracket is going up.

222 DON'T ALWAYS DEDUCT 10 PERCENT OF YOUR ADJUSTED GROSS INCOME.

Sometimes you can make a profit on a casualty loss. Let's say that you bought some antique bottles for $500, and their value soared to $5,000. Then your dog knocked all of them off a shelf. Your insurance company paid you $5,000 for the loss of the bottles. You must declare the profit you made, $4,500, as a capital gain. But if you have other casualty losses, you can deduct them from the profit.

If you're tallying together your casualty gains and your losses, and your profits are greater, skip the 10 percent reduction (but not the $100 reduction). If losses exceed gains, though, the 10 percent rule goes back into effect.

223 TRY TO AVOID BEING TAXED ON A PROFIT.

Your autograph collection cost you $5,000. When it was stolen, it was worth $10,000. Your insurance company paid you $8,000. Yes, you may have to pay taxes on the $3,000 gain—just as if you had sold the collection for $8,000. But you can get around this if you replace or repair missing or damaged property within a specified time: beginning on the day of the loss and ending two years after the end of the tax year in which you were reimbursed. (You lost your autographs in January 1989; your insurance company reimbursed you in November 1989; you have until December 1991, to amass an autograph collection of similar value.)

You need not report a gain if you're reimbursed with property similar to what was destroyed—even if its value exceeded your basis. Example: Your local moving company replaces your missing furniture with more valuable furniture.

224 DEDUCT APPRAISAL COSTS AS A MISCELLANEOUS EXPENSE.

List any fee you paid an appraiser—to establish your casualty-loss deduction—as a miscellaneous expense, not subject to the $100/10 percent of adjusted-gross-income reductions. But let's hope that your other miscellaneous deductions put you over the 2 percent floor for such expenses.

What if you pay an appraiser, then determine that you can't deduct a dime for casualty losses—because they didn't exceed 10 percent of your adjusted gross income? You're nonetheless allowed to deduct the cost as miscellaneous expense (above 2 percent of your adjusted gross income).

225 REMEMBER THAT FLORA HAVE VALUE.

You may not have paid extra for the trees, bushes, and plants on your property when you bought them, but they contributed to the value of your house. And it doesn't matter that you don't know their original cost. Find out what the property was worth before you lost any trees or shrubs, and afterward. The difference is your loss.

226 DON'T WAIT TO CLAIM A LOSS.

You can't afford to replace your car, or your furniture, or your clothing right now? Deduct the loss anyway. In fact, you *must* claim the loss in the year in which it occurred; you cannot delay, except when it's a question of your just discovering a loss (the theft of silverware a year ago, for example), or your trying to salvage something (trees you nursed, but that finally died three years after a freeze).

Chapter Seven
CHARITABLE
CONTRIBUTIONS

Don't just shrug off charitable contributions you've made. According to the IRS, they are the sixth-biggest way people lower their taxes.

But you may have a harder time deducting them now. Thanks to Tax Reform '86, you can no longer deduct charitable contributions unless you itemize your deductions on Schedule A, instead of taking the standard deduction.

In brief, the rules on charitable deductions are:

YOU CANNOT DEDUCT MORE THAN 50 PERCENT OF YOUR ADJUSTED GROSS INCOME IN ONE YEAR. But few people give that much.

YOU CANNOT DEDUCT CONTRIBUTIONS OF MORE THAN 20 PERCENT OF YOUR ADJUSTED GROSS INCOME IN ONE YEAR IF THE ORGANIZATION DOESN'T NORMALLY RECEIVE MUCH SUPPORT FROM THE PUBLIC OR FROM THE GOVERNMENT.

Example: a private foundation. This 20 percent limit also applies to gifts of long-term capital-gains property to veterans' organizations, fraternal societies, nonprofit cemetery companies, and private foundations. If in doubt, check with the organization. But, again, even 20 percent of your adjusted gross income is a big slice, so you probably don't have to worry.

YOU CANNOT DEDUCT MORE THAN 30 PERCENT OF YOUR ADJUSTED GROSS INCOME IN ONE YEAR IF YOU'RE GIVING LONG-TERM CAPITAL-GAINS PROPERTY. Here, we're talking about giving to charities that ordinarily qualify for the 50 percent limit. Example: You bought 100 shares of a stock you bought at 50; you're donating them at 100. You can deduct $10,000—so long as $10,000 isn't more than 30 percent of your adjusted gross income. And that would be unlikely for most people.

If you gave more than $500, not in cash but in property, you must fill out Form 8283.

If you gave $3,000 or more to any one organization, you must list the gift separately, and identify the organization.

If you made a contribution of over $5,000 and it was *not* either (a) cash or (b) stocks or other publicly traded securities, you must get a signed acknowledgment from the charity. (It's easy to establish the price of stocks traded among the public.) If you've made similar gifts during the year—shares of one stock, for example—they will be lumped together, and you may thus exceed the $5,000 limit.

With any gift over $5,000 (other than money or publicly traded securities), you'll also need a written professional appraisal, made within sixty days of your making the gift. (Otherwise, its value may have suddenly plummeted.) Try to get an appraisal early, because appraisers become busy at tax time. And without a note from an appraiser, your gift simply isn't tax-deductible.

The cost of an appraisal isn't deductible as a charitable expense but as a miscellaneous deduction.

As for saving taxes on charitable contributions, we'll begin with a familiar piece of advice:

227 BUNCH YOUR CHARITABLE CONTRIBUTIONS.

You can now deduct charitable gifts only if you itemize. So, if you've a mind to, try to contribute more than usual in years when you think you'll be able to itemize, less in the preceding or following years. At the same time, of course, this strategy may *enable* you to itemize in alternate years.

Let's say that you normally give $2,000 a year to churches, United Way, and so forth. If you're sure you'll be able to itemize this year, but possibly not next year, consider giving your usual $2,000 this year—and, at the close of the year, giving the $2,000 you would have contributed next year.

228 DON'T INCLUDE SCHEDULED DIVIDENDS.

Let's say that you give stock to a charity a few days before the stock will pay its regular dividend. Is the dividend excluded from the gift? No, a court has ruled.

229 DON'T DEDUCT FOR THE RIGHT TO USE YOUR PROPERTY.

A church is holding a raffle, and you auction off the right to use your vacation home for a week. Can you deduct the fair rental value as a contribution? No, the right to use property doesn't qualify. Nor could the successful bidder get a deduction: He or she received a "valuable" consideration for the money.

Okay, does the one-week use of the home by the bidder count as business use or personal use by you? Personal use, because the house wasn't *rented*.

230 DEDUCT 15 PERCENT TO ONE-THIRD THE ORIGINAL COST OF USED CLOTHING.

Tax experts say that these percentages are safe. But remember that you're entitled to deduct only the fair market value.

231 DEDUCT FOR A GIFT IN SOMEONE ELSE'S NAME.

Let's say that a couple are getting married and they suggest you make a contribution to their favorite charity in their name. You yourself can deduct the contribution—they can't (unless you give them the money, and they donate it).

232 DON'T OVERLOOK SMALL EXPENSES.

"People are always forgetting party refreshments they've sprung for, long-distance calls they've made, and auto expenses—such as for driving Girl Scouts around," says CPA Janice Johnson.

233 REMEMBER YOUR CASH CONTRIBUTIONS.

The cash you contribute—to a church or synagogue, to someone who rings your doorbell collecting for the Girl

Scouts or an environmental group—is deductible. Ideally, you will have kept records—not just to remind you, but to prove your contribution. Canceled checks or receipts are perfect. But the IRS notes that, in the case of small donations, you might produce "items such as buttons, tokens, or emblems that are given to contributors."

Even if you don't have canceled checks or receipts, you may still win the day. One man couldn't prove all his donations to a church, but a court was willing to take his word. The poor man had just been through his second divorce, the court noted, and as so often happens during times of stress, he "looked for solace in the church." Another man's estranged wife testified to support his undocumented deductions—which was nice of her.

The fact that any person has made generous, documented contributions to charities will help support his or her claims for undocumented contributions.

234 PLEDGE PART OF YOUR HOUSE.

Now taxpayers can irrevocably pledge a part of their homes to charity and get a charitable deduction for every year until they die. (Providing, of course, that they can itemize.) This tactic would be especially suitable for older people with no heirs, or with heirs who are prosperous.

The IRS has ruled that donors can pledge only a part of their homes (like 10 percent) to charity or to a nonprofit organization, and still qualify for a deduction. (In legalese, this is a "remainder interest in a residence"; the donors and the charity become "tenants in common.")

The donors can continue living in the house until they die. Then the house might be sold and the designated portion of the proceeds given to the charity. Or the heirs might give the charity cash, and keep the home. Or the donors might have bought life insurance to pay off their pledge.

The gift, once pledged, cannot be taken back. If the homeowners decide to move, the percentage of the house's value promised to charity can be passed along at the time of the sale.

The gift need not be a main residence. It could be a vacation home, or even raw land.

The yearly deduction the donors might get depends on their life expectancies. The older they are, the higher their yearly deduction. Donors might be best advised to make such gifts in years when their other deductions push them over the standard deduction ($5,200 for a couple filing jointly in 1989, $6,400 for a couple over sixty-five).

"This deferred giving," says Stuart M. Purchell, CPA, of San Rafael, California, "opens up a tremendous opportunity for older people, who may be worried about not having enough cash. Now they can contribute to charity and also enjoy tax benefits."

235 DON'T GIVE PROPERTY WITH LOSSES.

If you bought a stock at 100, and it's now 50, don't give it directly to a charity. Sell it first, then give the proceeds to the charity. That way, you can deduct the loss—either from your capital gains, or from your ordinary income (up to $3,000 a year).

236 GIVE PROPERTY WITH LONG-TERM GAINS.

If you contribute property—typically, stocks—that you owned for one year or less on the day you made the contribution, the profit is considered short-term, and your deduction is limited to what you paid for the property originally. Consider instead donating property that has long-term gains—that you've held for a year or more. The benefit: You won't be taxed on the appreciation. Giving $5,000 worth of property that includes appreciation on which you haven't paid taxes is better than giving $5,000 from your already-taxed income. But be warned that the appreciation may draw the alternative minimum tax upon you. (See Chapter 16.)

237 CARRY OVER ANY EXCESS CONTRIBUTIONS.

If you exceeded the limits on your contributions because they went above the specified percentage of your adjusted gross income, you can carry over the excess to the following year. For example, if your 1989 contributions were $10,000 and this was $1,000 more than half your adjusted gross income, your 1989 deduction is limited to $9,000. The unused $1,000 is added to your 1990 contributions, subject to the same percentage tests. You have five years to use up such excess charitable contributions.

238 DON'T ATTACH TIGHT STRINGS.

If you attach strings to your gift, you may not be allowed to deduct the value. Let's say you give a computer to a local high school, but you stipulate that you must be able to use it three months of the year. No deduction.

If the strings are loose, it's a different story. A man gave his town 800 acres of land, but wanted to keep training his dogs there. Deduction permitted. A deduction was also allowed with regard to a gift of manuscripts to the New York Public Library—despite the proviso that the manuscripts couldn't be copied without the permission of the gift-givers. If the amount is large, see a tax adviser.

239 GIVE BEFORE THE END OF THE YEAR.

You cannot deduct a pledge you make this year, promising to fork over the money or property next year. You'll have to wait until next year for your deduction.

240 WAIT UNTIL THE LAST MINUTE.

If you mail a contribution on December 31, you're considered to have made your gift that year—so long as you used a properly stamped and addressed envelope.

241 USE YOUR CREDIT CARD.

If you make a charitable contribution before the end of the year, by credit card, you can get a deduction for this year— and not have to pay the bill until it comes due. (But no, you don't get a deduction for a card that gives a charity a tiny fraction of whatever bills you run up.)

242 DON'T ASSUME ANY GIFT ISN'T DEDUCTIBLE.

You can deduct

• gifts to or for the use of a state, a territory, the United States, or a political subdivision
• gifts to a domestic fraternal or sororal society if used exclusively for religious or charitable purposes

• gifts to groups that try to prevent cruelty to children or animals, or that campaign for tolerance of homosexuals or spread information about women's rights

• gifts to promote national sports competitions if the group doesn't use any of its money to provide athletic facilities or equipment (but your contributions are deductible if given to certain *amateur* sports organizations that provide athletic facilities or equipment).

The gamut ranges from volunteer fire departments—to a state collecting for a parade to accompany a presidential inauguration.

You can even deduct a contribution to reduce the public debt and balance the budget. Submit a check made out to "Bureau of the Public Debt" when you send the IRS your tax return.

In one case, a contribution to a committee to commission a portrait of a new judge for display in a courthouse was held to be deductible.

So is a gift to a nonprofit cemetery corporation to support perpetual maintenance—so long as it's not for perpetual care of a particular lot (like yours).

When in doubt about whether your contribution is deductible, ask the organization. Don't assume anything. Even a group that tries to influence legislation may be considered a bona fide charity.

243 DON'T GIVE A VALUABLE PAINTING TO A TV STATION.

Give it to an art museum. For you to deduct the full value of your gift, it must be presented to a group that will use the gift in the course of its ordinary tax-exempt business. Otherwise, your deduction is limited to your gift's original cost.

Even if you present a painting to an art museum, you may be able to deduct only its original cost—if the museum sells your painting within two years. So, when you make such a gift, check what the group plans to do with your present—and get it in writing.

244 TAKE A DEDUCTION EVEN IF YOU BENEFIT A BIT.

A man was allowed to deduct a gift to a church—even though the church employed his wife. A doctor was permitted to deduct a lavish gift to a hospital although his generosity clearly helped brighten his reputation in the community. And a couple were allowed to deduct contributions to a church even though their son was the church's founder, minister, and president.

Said one judge, "Community goodwill, the desire to avoid community bad will, public pressures of other kinds, tax avoidance, prestige, conscience-salving, a vindictive desire to prevent relatives from inheriting family wealth—these are a few of the motives which may lie close to the heart, or so-called heart, of one who gives to charity." But motives don't matter, said the court.

If your motives are just a bit too obvious, though, you may be wiser to take your deduction as a business expense. Example: A cement maker gave to a YMCA's building fund—and he admitted he wanted the YMCA to use *his* cement. He took a business deduction.

245 DON'T BE TOO IMAGINATIVE.

Parents contributed to their two sons' support while the kids were unpaid church missionaries, and they took a charitable deduction. Deduction disallowed.

246 DON'T THINK THAT ONLY CASH OR CHECKS ARE DEDUCTIBLE.

You can also deduct the cost of clothing, household articles, supplies, and so forth. (To establish their fair market value, try to find what similar items have been selling for recently. If your gift is more than $500, remember, you must fill out Form 8283, and you may need an appraisal.)

One man bought a series of dancing lessons. He contributed them to a charity—and deducted what he had paid. Some landowners have been permitted charitable deductions for stipulating that nothing could be built on their land that would block off the scenic view of the area (a stipulation that lowered the value of their land).

Your own labor, though, is never deductible.

247 DEDUCT THE COST OF TRANSPORTATION.

If you use your car to help out a charitable, religious, or educational group—let's say you drive your Boy Scout group to a baseball game—you can deduct the cost of gas, repairs, tolls, and parking fees. But you can't deduct the cost of depreciation or auto insurance. If you don't want to figure out what percentage of your car's yearly use and expense went to charity, just multiply the mileage you used the car for charity by 12 cents (check that the number hasn't changed). You can then *add* parking fees and tolls.

Tax reform cracked down on away-from-home trips, purportedly to help a charity, that were really pleasure trips. (Now no deduction is permissible if you enjoyed a significant element of personal pleasure, recreation, or vacation.) Tax reform also cracked down on situations where a taxpayer gives $2,000 to a charity, and the charity pays that person to take a "fact-finding trip" in a resort area.

248 DEDUCT THE COST OF INCIDENTALS.

A volunteer nurse can deduct the cost and upkeep of his or her uniform if he or she paid for it and it's not something that person could wear elsewhere. The same is true for a Scoutmaster.

249 CHECK INTO THE DEDUCTIBILITY OF CONTRIBUTIONS TO INDIVIDUALS.

Usually, gifts to individuals aren't deductible—the $5 you give to someone who's homeless, for example. But a good Samaritan who provided lodging, food, and clothing to the victims of a hurricane, under the umbrella of various charitable organizations, was allowed to deduct his costs. Also deductible are reasonable costs for meals and recreation for a child's temporary care if the child was referred by a tax-exempt charitable organization. And a check to a certain missionary was deductible—because the money was for general missionary work.

You can deduct up to $50 per school month for a student—not a dependent or relative—who lives with you. You must have a written agreement with a qualifying organization, like a foreign-exchange group, and you cannot be reimbursed—unless it's for an unusual event, like the student's stay in a hospital. The student cannot be in college—just in the twelfth grade or lower. Money you spend for the student's books, food, clothing, tuition, and entertainment qualify.

250 GIVE A GROUP GIFT.

If you collect, say, books by one author, see if other collectors will join you in a gift of that author's books to a library.

The value of your gifts, together, will probably be more than the value of the gifts individually. That way, all of you may be able to take greater deductions.

Another example: Three different people gave three parcels of property to a nearby church. The value of the gifts together, divided by three, was worth more than the gifts had the parcels been given separately.

251 DEDUCT DUES...

along with membership fees, initiation fees, the cost of pew seats, or assessments if they went to a religious group. (But not if they went to a veterans' organization, country club, or other social group.)

252 DEDUCT THE DIFFERENCE BETWEEN THE COST OF A BENEFIT OVER THE REGULAR PRICE.

Ask the sponsors of the event what regular tickets would have cost. If two theater (or sports or film) tickets cost $40 ordinarily, and you paid $100, you can deduct $60. (You cannot deduct raffle tickets at all—unless you paid more than the regular price.) By the same token, you can deduct the difference between the price you pay for an annuity from a tax-exempt group and the annuity's fair market value.

If you buy a ticket to a benefit, and decline to accept the ticket—or donate it back to the charity, or to another charity—you can deduct the full cost.

Chapter Eight
SECURITIES

Tax reform all but eliminated the favored tax treatment of capital gains—the profits you reap by selling assets such as a stock, a house, a stamp collection, gold, or whatever. This is a drastic change. Ever since 1921, the tax code had treated capital gains ever so gently.

Now (unless Congress changes the rules) long-term gains (profit on assets you've owned more than a year) are taxed just the way your salary is—which could be as high as 33 percent. In the good old days (before 1987), the highest rate that long-term gains were taxed at was 20 percent.

In any case, the people who wrote the tax reform act expressly mentioned the possibility that someday capital gains will once again be treated like a favored child.

To refresh your memory:

If you sold any "capital assets" (gold, stocks, bonds, land) during the year, you must fill out Schedule D. After balancing losses and gains, you put the net gain or loss from your sale or exchange of capital assets on Form 1040. (Net losses are limited to $3,000 a year.)

Losses you have because of selling *personal* items aren't deductible at all. Examples: cars, boats, and houses that you don't use in your business. But you can use losses on *capital assets* to offset your gains, or even against $3,000 a year of your ordinary income if you don't have other capital gains.

Profits you've made from selling personal items *are* taxable. (I know. It doesn't seem fair.)

Long-term gains are those on assets you've owned over a year. (If you acquired the assets before 1988, long-term gains and losses are those on assets you had held over six months.)

To calculate your net gains or losses, on Schedule D you balance long-term gains against long-term losses; balance short-term gains against short-term losses. Then you offset net long-term gains or losses against net short-term gains or losses.

An important change that tax reform made: You can now use 100 percent of your long-term losses to offset short-term gains, or up to $3,000 a year of ordinary income.

The rule used to be that only 50 percent of long-term losses could be applied against gains, while short-term losses could offset gains, or up to $3,000 a year of ordinary income, dollar for dollar.

If your losses exceed $3,000 a year, carry over what's left to future years. You must use up short-term carryover losses before long-term losses, and earlier losses before later losses.

253   IF CAPITAL GAINS TAXES ARE CUT, RESTRUCTURE YOUR PORTFOLIO.

Ask yourself: Is the main reason that you've been holding any security the fact that you would owe gigantic taxes if you sold? That's not a good enough reason. Use any capital-gains cut as an impetus to create the very best portfolio you can.

254 TAKE NET GAINS IN THE YEAR YOUR BRACKET IS LOWER.

If you expect to be in the 15 percent bracket in 1990, for example, and the 28 percent bracket in 1991, and you have no good investment reason to take your gains in either year, shoot for 1990.

255 DEDUCT FOR WORTHLESS SECURITIES.

To establish a tax loss, you must usually sell or exchange your securities. If your stocks or bonds are almost worthless, ask a broker to buy them from you for a pittance.

With completely worthless securities, you can deduct your loss without selling them if you can prove they became worthless during that year. They are treated as if they had been sold on the last day of the year.

You can deduct the loss only in the year the security became completely worthless. To prove it, have evidence that the issuer is in bankruptcy, the company is in liquidation, or its normal business operations have stopped.

You have seven years to claim refunds on worthless securities on an amended return, despite the usual three-year statute of limitations.

256 SELL FOR A LOSS, AND BUY SOMETHING SIMILAR.

Let's say that you have a paper loss, and for tax reasons you want to nail down the loss in the current year. You can sell the stock, and buy it back thirty-one or more days later—or buy more shares at least thirty days before you sell the security. (If you or a blood relative bought it back any sooner, you couldn't deduct the loss. It would be a "wash sale.") Or sell the security and buy a similar but not "substantially identical" security. That way, you don't have to wait thirty-one days—during which time your stock may soar. If you sell Potomac Electric and buy Hawaii Electric, there's no wash sale; but if you sell a stock and buy the same company's preferred stock, your loss is washed out, and you cannot deduct it. You need never worry about the wash-sale rule if you sell a mutual fund for a loss and buy a similar fund. You could sell Nicholas and buy Nicholas II without being stung by the wash-sale rule because the two funds hold different stocks.

If you buy an option on a stock you've sold, to purchase it back cheaply if it goes up, you're subject to the wash-sale rule if you bought the option within sixty-one days of selling the stock.

What if you give your child money to buy a security you've sold? If the child signs a note and pledges the security as collateral, you can probably deduct the loss even if the child acquired it within sixty-one days of your selling it.

Another technique: doubling up. You own one hundred shares of XYZ, you have a loss, but you think the stock will go up. So you buy another one hundred shares, wait thirty days, and sell your original shares. Result: a tax loss and you still have the stock. You'll have commission costs, though.

257 POSTPONE A GAIN.

You can defer paying capital-gains taxes by selling a security short. That means borrowing the security from someone, selling it, then replacing it later on with the security you own (or will buy). The danger here is that the security's price will increase in the interim—and that you may owe dividends. But if you think the stock has appreciated enough, it may be worth it.

Let's say that you short your XYZ shares at the end of 1990. In January of 1991, you deliver the XYZ shares you owe. By delivering the stock in 1991, you postpone the sale—for tax purposes—until 1991.

258 CONSIDER BUYING ON MARGIN.

That means buying securities by borrowing money from your broker. You can deduct all of the interest up to the income you receive from your securities, plus 20 percent of the excess, up to $2,000 more (in 1989) or 10 percent of the excess, up to $1,000 more (in 1990). You can borrow 50 percent of the stocks you buy, 70 percent on bonds, and up to 90 percent on Treasury obligations.

The interest rate you'll pay your broker will be competitive. You'll pay a higher rate on debts up to around $50,000.

The danger is that your purchases may go down, and you'll be subject to a "margin call"—a demand that you fork over more cash. If you don't have the cash, your securities will be sold, giving you an automatic loss. Buying on margin is only for sophisticated investors.

259 CUT YOUR LOSSES AND LET YOUR WINNERS RIDE.

This is an investing truism, and it makes sense for tax reasons, too. The quicker you take losses, the higher your deductions—and the more money you'll have left to invest, save, or spend. And now that you can deduct 100 percent of your long-term losses against gains, and against $3,000 of ordinary income every year, you have more incentive to weed out your losers.

The slower you take gains, the lower your overall tax bill—and, again, the more money you'll have left to do with as you please.

As an investment strategy it makes sense, too. If a stock of yours nosedives, there's a chance that other investors know something you don't—for example, that the company's sales are turning sour. But if a stock of yours declines along with the market, and your reasons for buying it still apply, you might be wiser to hold on. On balance, it's probably better to sell stocks or other securities if they've fallen 10 percent or 15 percent below your purchase price— partly because of the psychological temptation to hold on, and thus not admit to yourself that you made a mistake buying it in the first place.

If a stock of yours has climbed, it's usually a good idea to hold on, too. Stocks have momentum. If a company's earnings have risen and business is booming, you can expect the company to continue doing well for a while. But if the stock is a small-company stock, as opposed to a blue chip (older, bigger company), it's probably quite volatile. And big ruthless companies may move in to swipe the small company's booming business. You might be more inclined to sell such stocks to lock in your gains.

But don't try to sell out at the exact point when a stock reaches its all-time high. Hardly anyone can do that successfully, time after time. Even the legendary investor Bernard Baruch said, "I always sold too soon."

Granted, many investors do hold stocks too long. They buy a stock at 20, watch it go to 30, and then can't sell— because they greedily hope it will go to 40. They watch in growing dismay as the stock drops back to 20, or even lower, and their profits slip away. As the stock sinks, they become depressed—and, like depressed people in general, they can't act—they can't call their broker and say, "Sell!"

But probably it's even more common for investors to sell too soon. They make a small profit, then hurry to the exit. They continually violate the rule "Sell your losers and let your winners ride"; they hold on to their losers and cut back on their winners. A bank trust officer I know tells me, "Families that have made fortunes have bought good stocks, and held on year after year."

If you simply can't decide whether to sell or hold on, the best solution may be: Sell half your holdings.

As an overall strategy, holding on to your winners makes even more sense, thanks to tax reform.

Beginning in 1988, people have been saying, capital gains will be taxed just like ordinary income—your salary, for instance. But that's not quite true. An advantage that capital gains still have over ordinary income is that you needn't pay any taxes on them until you actually cash in your assets. And if you hold your gains until you die, your heirs will inherit your holdings—and *their* cost basis for the assets will generally be the price of the assets on the day you died. (Or, if they choose, six months after your death.) So all of your capital gains—accumulated year after year—can escape taxes. That is one heck of an advantage that capital gains have over ordinary income!

But like all investing rules, there are exceptions. Do sell an asset on which you have a profit if you think that its long-term prospects are dim. Putting a stock in a drawer and never looking at it again isn't appropriate anymore, if it ever once was. Those investors who believe in holding on forever may wind up owing shares of companies that went bankrupt years ago.

260 DON'T FORGET THE CAPITAL LOSS CARRYOVER.

Check your last year's tax return, Schedule D, to see whether you had capital losses you couldn't entirely use up. These unused losses can be deducted from your current year's capital gains, or from up to $3,000 of ordinary income. (Losses retain their status as long-term or short-term. Even if you have carryover losses from before 1987, they can offset ordinary income dollar for dollar.) You can continue to use carryover losses until they're used up, or until you die.

261 ADD BROKERS' COMMISSIONS TO YOUR COST.

When you calculate your gains or losses, add the broker's commission to your basis (total investment). That will lower your taxable gains or raise your deductible losses. If you reinvested dividends to buy more stock, add the small fees that your company charged you. (And remember to use the purchase prices of those shares in calculating your total profits or losses.) The broker's commissions when you sell are deducted from your sales price, and will also reduce your taxable gains.

262 DECIDE WHETHER YOU WANT HIGH OR LOW TAXABLE GAINS.

You can—if you bought shares at different times. You can then sell older certificates or newer ones. Usually the older certificates will have the higher gains. But you could have purchased the newer ones when they were real bargains, and thus their gains could be higher.

In a typical situation, an investor needs money, and wants

to sell some of his or her holdings. The investor should sell the most costly shares, and thus incur the lower taxes.

But you may want higher gains this year if your tax rate will climb next year, or you have lots of losses to offset against your gains.

Or you may want lower gains now because your tax rate will sink next year, or you need money and have no losses to offset against them.

If you simply sell your shares, without instructing your broker which to sell (if the broker holds them), or by sending in certificates at random, the IRS will decide that you sold the certificates you bought first. (First in, first out.) With a mutual fund, you don't usually receive certificates. To adjust your gains or losses, instruct the fund or its transfer agent to sell shares you bought on a particular date.

263 SELL LOSING FUNDS, KEEP WINNERS.

With stock mutual funds, it's probably an even wiser approach to cut your losses and let your winners ride. Afraid that a mutual fund that's done well has overpriced stocks, poised for a fall? The portfolio manager may have been smart enough to have sold his or her winners and bought other, undervalued, stocks—although the fund's quarterly report doesn't show the switches yet. Hopeful that a fund that's plummeted has underpriced stocks, ready for a rise? The manager may have panicked, sold those low-priced stocks, and purchased recent winners—which are now overpriced.

264 DEDUCT A SALES COMMISSION NOW.

Here's how. You want to buy Fidelity Magellan, which has a 3 percent sales charge. So you buy Fidelity Overseas, which also has a 3 percent sales charge. Then you instruct the Fidelity family to sell your shares of Overseas, and switch them into Magellan. Result: You have a 3 percent loss on Overseas, which you can deduct this year.

You can do this with any fund family that doesn't charge you for switching among its funds.

265 CONSIDER SELLING IF YOU HAVE A PHANTOM TAX LOSS.

You buy shares of a fund and soon get a distribution—an enormous one, because the fund has been doing so well. That distribution, plus your shares' cost, may boost your tax basis to such an extent that you have a tax loss. Consider selling and switching to a similar fund.

266 DON'T BUY SHARES RIGHT BEFORE A DISTRIBUTION.

If you send in your investment just before a distribution of capital gains, dividends, or interest, you'll suddenly have taxes to pay on the distribution you've received. This is especially undesirable if you paid in a large amount, and thus received a large taxable distribution. Telephone the fund before you invest, find out when it goes "ex-dividend" (the date when current shareholders are entitled to distributions), and wait a few days after that before buying shares. The distribution may be made a few days after the ex-dividend date. (Many funds make distributions in December.)

267 REMEMBER TO DEDUCT COMMISSIONS.

If you sold mutual funds with either front-end commissions or redemption fees, deduct them from your gains—or add them to your losses.

268 BUY A FUND WITH A LOW TURNOVER.

Such a fund doesn't buy and sell much, so you won't have a lot of capital-gains taxes to pay (assuming the fund's stocks rise). So, if two funds you're considering have similar performance records, pay attention to how frequently the fund trades its shares. The typical fund has a turnover of about 100 percent—in effect, it replaces all its holdings during one year.

269 REMEMBER THE ADVANTAGES OF TREASURY OBLIGATIONS.

First, their interest is not taxed by state and local governments. And second, you can defer the taxation on the interest you earn on securities that come due in one year or less—if you buy an obligation that matures next year, not this. Buy a one-year Treasury bill in January and you won't receive your interest until next January—and you won't have to pay taxes on your interest until April of next year.

Of course, Treasuries also happen to be the safest investment in the world, and the interest they pay isn't bad, either. You can usually buy a high-grade corporate bond that pays more, but the interest will be subject to Federal, state and local taxes. (And if the company is taken over, your high-grade bond may become low grade.) Municipal bonds usually pay less, but they're usually exempt from *Federal* taxes, too. Still, both corporates and munis may be called in before they come due. Treasuries are very rarely called.

Treasury *bills* are short-term, Treasury *notes* are intermediate-term, and Treasury *bonds* are long-term.

The least expensive T-bill is $10,000; beyond that, bills are issued in multiples of $5,000. They mature (come due) in three, six, or twelve months. The longer the maturity, usually the higher interest they pay—and the greater the risk that you'll be locked in if interest rates in general rise. But while the Treasury Department won't cash in your obligations before maturity, you can sell them early through a bank or broker—at a discount.

All Treasury bills (with a one-year maturity or less) are sold to you at a discount, too. The difference between what you buy them for, and their face value, is your interest—as is true of Series EE savings bonds. For example, if the interest rate on a one-year bill is 10 percent, you can buy a bond with a $10,000 face value, immediately get $1,000 returned to you, and then receive $10,000 a year later.

You can buy Treasury obligations through banks or brokers for a fee ($25 is typical). You can also buy them directly from a branch of the Federal Reserve near you. For an application, write to the Bureau of the Public Debt, Department of the Treasury, Washington, DC 20239.

Treasury notes usually have maturities from two to ten years. Those maturing in less than four years have minimum denominations of $5,000; those maturing in four years or more, $1,000. Interest is paid twice a year.

Treasury bonds have maturities extending from over ten years to thirty years. Minimum denomination: $1,000. Interest is paid twice a year.

Check before paying state taxes on dividends from mutual funds that invest in U.S. Treasury obligations. Your state may exempt the funds. Check with the fund.

270 DON'T OVERLOOK SERIES EE BONDS.

Remember when savings bonds were low-paying, dull investments? No more.

Today, Series EE savings bonds are hot items. One reason: The interest may be tax exempt if the bonds were issued on or after January 1, 1990, and you use the interest to pay certain educational expenses. See the Introduction for the rules. Another reason: The interest is exempt from state and local taxes, which have been climbing. Another: Their earnings can be tax-deferred. Finally, if inflation returns, the interest on Series EE bonds may keep apace because the rates are changed every six months, in line with the rates on five-year Treasury securities.

Savings bonds have become an especially good purchase for children, now that family income-shifting possibilities have been cut back. You can buy bonds for a two-year-old child, in the child's name, and cash them in when the child is fourteen or older. At that time, their accumulated interest will be taxed at the child's low rates. Of course, if the child has little other investment income, there's no reason for the child to defer paying taxes on the bonds. Up to $500 of a child's unearned income is untaxed and up to $500 is taxed at the child's rate, not at the parents' rate. Note: Bonds bought in the child's name are not eligible for the tax exemption for tuition payments.

Series EE bonds are also suitable for someone nearing retirement: The would-be retiree can invest in the bonds, and get the entire accumulated interest when he or she retires and very likely is in a lower tax bracket.

EE bonds sell at a discount from their face value. A $50 bond, for instance, sells for $25. At maturity, you receive the $50.

You cannot buy Series EE bonds with a face value of more than $30,000 in any calendar year in any one person's name. You cannot use them as collateral for a loan. You cannot cash them in during the first six months.

To purchase savings bonds, visit banks, savings and loan associations, or Federal Reserve Banks, or buy them through your employer's payroll savings plan.

Don't confuse Series EE bonds with Series HH bonds, whose interest rate is fixed. HH bonds also provide current interest. You can buy Series HH bonds only with at least $500 of Series EE or the older E bonds. Unlike EE bonds, with HH bonds there's no reduction in the interest rate if you cash them in early.

The bonds mature in ten years, but the interest is reportable each year.

You can buy a bond on the last day of the month and receive interest from the first day of the month. (Yes, there are free lunches.)

As for redeeming bonds, remember that interest is credited every six months, counting from the month of purchase, for bonds held over nineteen months. Try to redeem bonds only after the latest six month period, to receive the full interest. If you need cash and have old as well as new savings bonds to sell, sell the newer ones if you've held them at least five years. Because your newer bonds have less accumulated interest, cashing them in won't add as much to your tax bill. (Bonds sold before five years earn less interest.)

271 DEFER PAYING TAXES ON SERIES EE BONDS PAST THEIR MATURITY.

You can, by using them to buy HH bonds, and thus postponing paying taxes on your accumulated Series EE earnings. You can hold the HH bonds until they mature in ten years, or until you decide to cash them in. With the older E bonds, you could just hold them past their maturity, and still postpone taxes on their accumulated interest.

272 BUY VARIOUS DENOMINATIONS OF SAVINGS BONDS.

If you cash in a bond before five years, the interest rate becomes very low. That's why you shouldn't buy a few bonds with high face values. Instead, buy a variety of smaller bonds, so that if you need money immediately, you won't have to cash in your big bonds and wind up with a low interest rate on a lot of money.

273 DON'T FORGET TO DEDUCT LOSSES . . .

if you sold corporate or municipal bonds for less than you bought them. The same goes for bonds you bought at a premium (above their original selling price): When they mature, you can deduct a loss. Or you can deduct a portion of the premium every year. By the same token, you must pay capital-gains taxes on your bonds if you sold them before they matured, for *more* than you paid.

You can avoid the wash-sale rule if you sell a bond at a loss and, within thirty-one days, buy a bond issued by the same company but with a very different interest rate. Just buying a bond issued by the same company but with a different *maturity* date is risky. You may not be able to deduct your loss.

274 CONSIDER SINGLE-STATE MUNI BONDS OR FUNDS.

If you live in a state with high state taxes (like New York, California, Ohio, Minnesota, and Maryland), consider a mutual fund that buys only municipals issued in your state. Your interest will escape state and local taxes as well as Federal taxes. For the names of such funds, contact the Investment Company Institute in Washington, DC.

States that tax out-of-state bonds but not within-the-state bonds include Alabama, Arizona, Arkansas, California (11 percent), Colorado, Connecticut, Delaware, Georgia, Hawaii, Idaho, Kansas, Kentucky, Louisiana, Maine, Maryland, Massachusetts, Michigan, Minnesota, Mississippi, Missouri, Montana, New Hampshire, New Jersey, New York, North Carolina, North Dakota, Ohio, Oklahoma, Oregon, Pennsylvania, Rhode Island, South Carolina, Tennessee, Virginia, and West Virginia.

Bonds issued by the territories—Puerto Rico, the U.S. Virgin Islands, and Guam—are exempt from taxes in most states. Talk with a stockbroker.

275   DECIDE WHAT INTEREST RATE WOULD APPEAL TO YOU.

To determine whether a tax-exempt or a taxable bond makes economic sense for you, check what taxable bonds (like corporates) are paying now, then estimate your top tax rate. If your top rate—your "marginal" rate—will be 28 percent in 1989, for example, a taxable bond would have to yield 11.11 percent to equal a muni yielding 8 percent.

Taxable Versus Tax-Exempt Bonds

To equal a municipal bond yielding:	5%	6%	7%	8%	9%
If you're in the 15 percent marginal tax bracket, a taxable bond must yield	5.88%	7.06%	8.24%	9.41%	10.59%
If you're in the 28 percent marginal tax bracket, a taxable bond must yield	6.94%	8.33%	9.72%	11.11%	12.5%
If you're in the 33 percent marginal tax bracket, a taxable bond must yield	7.46%	8.95%	10.44%	11.94%	13.4%

276 CONSIDER ZERO COUPON BONDS.

They can be ideal for pension plans like IRAs and for saving for a child's college education.

Zeros can be based on corporate bonds, Treasury obligations, or municipal bonds. They're fixed-income investments that don't pay you interest until the principal becomes due.

You can buy zeros at a small fraction of their eventual redemption value, which will include their principal as well as all the accumulated interest.

Although you won't receive interest on your zero bond, every year you'll have to pay taxes on the interest you've deferred.

You can purchase a $1,000 zero for as little as $100 or $200—the price depends on when it comes due and the yield. Because you must pay fees—2 percent to 5 percent of the purchase price—shop around among brokers and bankers for the best deal.

One benefit of zeros is that you know exactly how much you'll receive when they mature—whether in ten years or thirty years. Also, you don't have to decide how to reinvest the interest: You don't receive any until the zero comes due. Finally, a zero is a way to force yourself to save money.

Taxable zeros—from corporate bonds or Treasuries—are suitable for pension plans like IRAs and Keoghs, because you won't have to pay taxes on the "phantom" interest over the years (the interest you don't receive).

Tax-exempt zeros—based on municipal bonds—are suitable for saving for a child's college education. Even when they mature, you or your child won't owe any taxes.

One drawback of zeros is that, because they're long-term, their principal can fluctuate wildly over the years, depending on current interest rates. If you must cash them in early, and interest rates have climbed, you may be shocked at how much their value has sunk. Of course, if interest rates have gone down, you can cash in a zero early—at a profit.

Here's how to figure out how much you'll receive from zeros, if you're using them to finance a child's education:

Invest Now to Have $1,000 When a Child Reaches Eighteen

	YIELDS				
Age of Child	6%	7%	8%	9%	10%
Newborn	$345	$290	$244	$205	$173
Five-year-old	464	409	361	318	281
Ten-year-old	623	577	534	494	458

If you have a baby, and you want to provide $60,000 for the child's college education at age eighteen and your yield is 9 percent, you would buy sixty times $205, or $12,300, worth of zeros.

With a few corporate-bond zeros, you don't have to pay taxes on phantom interest. They include General Motors Acceptance Corporation bonds maturing in 2012 and 2015, and Exxon Shipping Company bonds of 2012.

Chapter Nine
INSURANCE

Making an investment through an insurance policy may seem peculiar, but it's been done for years. And now tax reform has helped make whole-life insurance, along with annuities, among the most seductive investments around.

Reason: These two insurance company products emerged from tax reform almost unscathed. The money you put into whole-life insurance or annuities can still appreciate year after year without being taxed.

If you're among those people who can't deduct an IRA contribution anymore, why not use an insurance investment to shield your retirement money from taxes? And why be limited to a piddling $2,000 a year when you can salt away as much as $5 million a year?

And because you no longer can move much money into your kids' low brackets to save for their college educations, why not sprinkle money into an insurance policy that lets you invest in a tax-shielded mutual fund—and borrow your investments at a low interest rate, or even free of charge?

If you think all this sounds too good to be true, you're right. Annuities and life insurance are glamorous, but they have sharp thorns.

• Comparing policies is dizzyingly difficult. The insurance industry hasn't standardized the provisions, and the possible permutations and combinations seem infinite.

• As a result, getting reliable advice is a problem. Even some of the very best financial planners say they're sticking to selling simple term insurance—because they don't understand all the other stuff.

• The policies themselves are strewn with hidden fees, even though they may be described as "no loads."

But at this point, let's pause for a somewhat oversimplified crash course in life insurance and annuities.

Once upon a time, you had mainly a choice between term and whole-life (also called cash-value) insurance. Term is pure insurance—plain vanilla, with no artificial flavoring. You don't make any kind of investment; the premiums rise as you grow older. Whole-life insurance, which costs far more, comes with a savings account. The premiums remain level.

The trouble with whole life is that (1) the sales charges can be enormous; (2) the savings account pays relatively little; and (3) the insurance company uses the cash value to keep the premium unchanging. So, when you die, your beneficiaries receive only the face amount of the policy. (If you borrow your cash value, your insurance coverage is reduced.) And the fact that the premiums don't rise isn't really helpful. The young need lots of insurance, not high premiums; older people can better afford higher premiums, but—in any case—usually need less life insurance.

"Universal" life insurance is an improved version of cash-value insurance. The savings account grows at a competitive interest rate. And you have a lot of flexibility:

You can allot your premiums between the cash value and insurance, and even change the size and frequency of your premiums. But even with most universal-life policies, your savings account is lost if you die.

"Variable" life insurance entered the scene in 1976. Here, your savings account fluctuates according to market conditions—your return isn't fixed. The reason is that your money can be invested in a variety of mutual funds, including stock funds, depending upon your choice. (This is somewhat risky, but the stock market is where big money can be made.)

While your heirs don't receive the cash value of a variable policy when you die, your insurance coverage grows in step with the cash value. So you don't lose all of your appreciation if you die while holding onto the policy: The policy's face value reflects the appreciation.

Another innovation is "single premium" variable life insurance. You invest a lump sum—as little as $5,000 or as much as $5 million, but typically $50,000 or so. Depending on your age, your premium buys two to ten times the amount in insurance protection. Now Congress has imposed a 10 percent penalty, however, if you borrow from your investment early on.

Annuities have also undergone major changes. Once they were just a form of insurance that protected you in case you lived as long as Methuselah. You paid in your money, and later on you received a yearly stipend, as long as you lived—even if the insurance company lost money on the deal. Their key drawback was that the stipend could be shrunk by inflation. But now you can buy not just flexible-interest annuities—those that regularly change their interest rates—but variable annuities, attached to stock mutual funds. Despite their volatility, they can keep your assets in line with normal inflation.

Unfortunately, you cannot borrow from an annuity without owing income taxes.

Obviously, whole-life insurance and annuities are well worth considering—but you must make some difficult choices.

277 LOOK FOR INSURANCE PRODUCTS WITH LOW SALES CHARGES.

Among those mentioned by financial planners: American Life of New York (212-581-1200); Bankers Life Nebraska (800-255-9678); Essex (201-325-3655); Lincoln Benefit (800-525-9287); USAA (800-531-8000). In a recent poll of fee-only financial planners, USAA was clearly the favorite.

278 CONSIDER INSURANCE-BASED INVESTMENTS RATHER THAN A MUNI FUND.

Both a municipal-bond fund and insurance-based investments provide tax-free or tax-deferred accumulations.

A muni-bond fund has certain advantages. You can get your money out quickly, and without special penalties. (With the insurance policies, the company may hit you with a surrender charge if you withdraw your investment in the first few years.) And if you withdraw your money from a muni fund, you won't owe taxes on the interest.

But with the insurance products, you may get a higher return. The insurer can invest in high-paying corporate bonds, for example, as well as stocks. Also, if you die, the proceeds of both annuities and life insurance escape the costs of probate courts. With annuities, your heirs owe income taxes only on the appreciation; with life insurance, all proceeds are untaxed. That's not the case with a muni fund or other investments.

Of course, there's nothing wrong with having both a muni fund and insurance investments.

279 CONSIDER A VARIABLE ANNUITY IF YOU'RE YOUNG.

Younger people might opt for a variable annuity, choosing greater risk for possibly greater rewards. At their age, they can wait out any stock-market declines. Older people might lean toward a fixed annuity, because they might need money just when the stock market is in the doldrums. Again, there's no rule against having both types of annuities.

280 CONSIDER VARIABLE INSURANCE ALONG WITH NO-LOAD MUTUAL FUNDS.

Most no-load funds have lower expenses and fees than variable annuities and variable life. But the insurance-linked funds do protect your profits from taxes—year after year, until withdrawn.

Another disadvantage of insurance-linked mutual funds: Comparing their records isn't easy. Most newspapers don't publish them. Still, if your fund has performed poorly, you can usually transfer to sister money-market or bond funds; you can even switch from one insurance company's policy to another, without tax consequences.

All in all, it's probably best to diversify—to have some of your funds in no-load funds and some in variable insurance policies and variable annuities.

281 CHOOSE INSURANCE PRODUCTS CAREFULLY.

Buy from insurance companies rated A+ by the A.M. Best Company. Check a library for Best's Reports, or ask insurance agents.

If you're purchasing a fixed and not a variable annuity, find out the initial interest rate, and see how long it's guaranteed. Inquire about early-withdrawal fees: You want them to vanish in a few years, not in ten years.

With a variable life, again look for policies from companies rated A or A+ by the A.M. Best Company (check Best's Reports in your library or ask your insurance agent), policies also allied with mutual funds run by top investment companies. American Funds in Los Angeles, Merrill Lynch, and Fidelity are among the better known investment companies linking mutual funds with variable insurance. (But any fund open to the general public cannot be offered in a variable policy, so you cannot buy—for example—a famous fund like Fidelity Magellan via an insurance policy.)

Chapter Ten
INVESTMENT
REAL ESTATE

One reason why commercial real estate has been languishing of late is that tax reform sharply curtailed its benefits. Yet some advantages remain, and investors can still profit from them.

To begin with, we'll offer tips on how to cope with the changes. Then we'll relay some time-honored strategies that still work, despite tax reform. Many of the suggestions were provided by Martin M. Shenkman, a lawyer in New York City and Teaneck and the co-author of *How to Buy a Home with No (Or Little) Money Down*, published by John Wiley & Sons.

282 DEPRECIATE LAND IMPROVEMENTS FASTER.

Improvements to land can be depreciated over just fifteen years. Examples: sidewalks, roads, drainage facilities, fences, certain landscaping and shrubbery.

Under tax reform, residential real estate put in use after 1986 must be depreciated over the course of 27.5 years, and other real estate over 31.5 years. Accelerated depreciation, which is more generous than straight-line depreciation, is no longer permitted on real property—except for land improvements.

283 AVOID PERMANENT IMPROVEMENTS, EMPHASIZE REPAIRS.

You cannot immediately deduct the cost of an improvement; all you can do is add it to your basis (total investment), and depreciate the cost. You can deduct the cost of repairs in the year you make them. That's why you should emphasize repairs.

True, the line between improvements and repairs can be narrow. In general, though, if you maintain your property the way you should, you are in the bailiwick of repairs—and you may not be forced to treat your expenditures as nondeductible improvements.

Consider sealing, patching, or repaving a driveway instead of installing a new one. Think about repairing your furnace or water heater instead of splurging on new models. Don't have a house renovated all at once: have it painted one year, new carpets installed the next, and new wallpaper put up the third year. If you have everything done at once, or in accordance with a renovation plan, the IRS may consider it an improvement, not a series of repairs.

284 DEPRECIATE PERSONAL PROPERTY FASTER.

You can still depreciate "personal property" over just five or seven years—faster than you can depreciate "real property." (Personal property: furniture, equipment, and such. Real property consists of the building and its structural parts.) And with personal property, you can still use accelerated depreciation—deducting more during the early years, less later on.

285 MAKE ANY ADDITIONS PERSONAL PROPERTY.

The key distinction is that personal property is easily movable. So, make your additions movable. Instead of nailing down a carpet or tiles, attach them with special removable glue. Put up a ready-made bookcase, not a built-in bookcase.

286 LEASE THE LAND.

If you buy a house or factory but rent the land, more of your investment can be depreciated. (Land cannot be depreciated.) And you can immediately deduct your rental payments for the land.

287 IF YOU EXPECT LOSSES, LOWER YOUR ADJUSTED GROSS INCOME TO BELOW $100,000.

Under tax reform, losses from rental property are deductible in full only from other "passive" income (like income from limited partnerships), not from "active" income (wages) and portfolio income (dividends and interest).

A key exception: If (a) your adjusted gross income is under $100,000, (b) you "actively" manage your property, and (c) you own at least 10 percent of the property, you can deduct up to $25,000 in real-estate losses against ordinary or portfolio income. (From $100,000 to $150,000, you lose the deductions at a rate of $1 for every $2 of income.) If you bought the property on or before October 22, 1986, you can deduct 20 percent of excess losses in 1989, 10 percent in 1990, and none in 1991 and afterward. Losses beyond these percentages can be carried over to succeeding years. When you have a profit in a particular year, or you sell, you can offset any gains with these carryover losses. If you sell for a loss, you can deduct the entire loss.

The maximum $25,000 deduction is, oddly enough, the same whether you are married or single. But if a married couple living together file separately, they lose the deduction. If they live apart and file separately, the deduction is cut in half. (The IRS wants to discourage marrieds from filing separate returns.)

So, if you expect to have nondeductible losses, try to keep your adjusted gross income below $100,000—by speeding up expenses, deferring income, and funding your deductible pension plans to the hilt, for example. (IRAs, in this case, won't lower your adjusted gross income.)

288   ... OR CUT YOUR LOSSES.

If your property losses stem from mortgage debt, for example, pay off the debt—so you may wind up with passive income, which you can write off against other passive losses. A good way to pay off the debt: Refinance your personal residences. You can deduct interest on a total $100,000 home-equity mortgage, plus your outstanding original mortgage with a $1.1 million limit.

289   DON'T THINK $25,000 IS THE LIMIT ...

on expenses you can deduct for rental property. The $25,000 limit is net—income minus losses. You can have $200,000 in rental income and deduct $225,000 in expenses (if you otherwise qualify).

290 TAKE A PARTIAL DEDUCTION FOR PROPERTY LOSSES . . .

if you contracted to buy real estate before October 22, 1986, even if the actual payment came later, so long as your agreement was binding.

291 LOWER YOUR INCOME IN ALTERNATE YEARS.

The result will be that, in those alternate years, you may be below the $100,000 floor. Postpone, or speed up, receiving income—from bonuses, commissions, sales, whatever. In 1990, you might try to accelerate income normally scheduled for 1991—because, in 1990, 10 percent of excess passive losses will be deductible from other kinds of income, versus nothing in 1991.

292 PROVE THAT YOU ACTIVELY MANAGE YOUR PROPERTY.

Even if you use a rental agent, you should approve new tenants, okay improvements or repair expenses over $100 or $200, decide on rental terms, sign original or renewal leases, keep copies of paperwork. You should also keep a folder in which you place notes about conversations with your agent or tenants, and visits to your property. If you're buying property, in the first place, it should be within an hour's drive, so you can more easily prove you're an active manager.

293 CONSIDER PIGS.

"Passive income generators," they're called. Limited partnerships that produce passive income. But be careful. Many PIGs being sold now are risky, or produce income that the IRS may consider nonpassive.

Master limited partnerships no longer produce passive income but portfolio income. And "working interests" in oil and gas drilling ventures escape the limitations on deducting your losses.

294 CONSIDER USING YOUR SUMMER HOME MORE.

If you have paper losses from renting a vacation home and you can no longer fully deduct them from nonpassive income, consider spending more time there yourself—more than fourteen days a year or 10 percent of the days it's rented. If it's your second residence, you may be able to deduct a greater portion of the property taxes and mortgage interest (if you itemize).

295 TRADE YOUR HOLDINGS.

Your ability to defer capital gains when you swap properties may be sharply curtailed: The House Ways and Means Committee wants to restrict tax-free exchanges to properties where the use is similar—no more swapping farms for condominiums, for example.

Even so, the rule can be useful—if the properties are really similar. Both properties must have been held for business or investment purposes. Your new mortgage must equal or exceed the mortgage on the property you're trading, or you will have to recognize some gain.

The property you're to receive must be identified within forty-five days of your transferring your own property. The exchange itself must be completed within 180 days after the transfer of the first property—or the extended due date of your tax return, if earlier.

Warning: If you've fully depreciated your own property, you cannot depreciate the new property.

296 CONSIDER AN INSTALLMENT SALE.

Why confine all your capital gains from selling your property to one year? Consider using the installment sale method. You can then spread the reporting of any gains, and paying taxes on them, over the course of time you receive the proceeds.

Note: In the year you sell the property, you may have to recapture any depreciation you've taken on the property—not as you receive the proceeds. And if you are considered a dealer in property, you will have to recognize all gain in the year of the sale.

297 DON'T DEPRECATE DEPRECIATION.

Depreciation is the regular deduction of the cost of a business asset over its lifetime because it's supposedly losing value as it grows older—like a typewriter you use in your work. If a business asset of yours has a five-year life (for tax purposes) you can deduct a fixed percentage of its value every year. (A typewriter supposedly has a five-year life.) This is called "straight-line" depreciation. If you could deduct a higher percentage during an asset's early years, and a lesser percentage later on, it would be "accelerated" depreciation. Accelerated is usually better; you save more money, sooner.

Most real estate appreciates; it doesn't actually depreciate—until it gets *very* old. So the depreciation deduction is just a special benefit that real-estate investors enjoy.

In the good old days, you could depreciate residential and commercial real estate over fifteen years. Tax reform has lengthened the time. Depreciation isn't what it used to be, but what's left should be very much appreciated.

298   BUYERS SHOULD EMPHASIZE INTEREST, NOT PRICE.

Thanks to tax reform, when you buy property now, it may be better to pay less for the property, and pay higher interest on any mortgage. Remember that now you must depreciate property over a longer period of time, using straight-line depreciation, whereas you can deduct interest payments much sooner.

As for sellers, with the distinction between capital gains and interest income being wiped out, whether they receive a higher price or higher interest may not matter.

299   START DEPRECIATING AS EARLY AS YOU CAN.

You needn't wait until a tenant actually moves in, or the day he or she signs the lease. When the building is available for rental, and you're trying to rent it, generally you can start depreciating it.

300   DELAY PURCHASES OF PERSONAL PROPERTY WHEN YOU'RE NEAR $200,000.

You can write off up to $10,000 for items of personal property you use in your business in the year you buy them.

This benefit is phased out, dollar for dollar, when your purchases exceed $200,000. (The $10,000 write-off is called "expensing" or the Section 179 deduction.)

So that you can continue to deduct up to $10,000, try to delay purchasing some assets to the early part of next year if you're nearing the $200,000 limit.

301 RENT TO A RELATIVE.

You'll still qualify for tax benefits, so long as the rent is set at or near the fair market value. You'll have a regular tenant who won't skip in the middle of the night; your relative will have a kind, gentle landlord.

302 DON'T OVERLOOK DEDUCTIBLE EXPENSES.

Besides depreciation, there's fire insurance, liability insurance, advertising for tenants, cleaning services, travel expenses (including meals and lodgings when you visit rental property outside your area), legal, architectural, and accounting fees, supplies, water, fuel, taxes.

Remember maintenance too—repainting, repapering, fixing leaks, repairing plumbing and wiring, extermination, and so forth.

303 DEDUCT RENTAL EXPENSES EVEN IF YOU DON'T ITEMIZE.

Use Schedule E to deduct your rental expenses from your rental income.

304   CONSIDER BUYING A VACATION HOME.

In some ways, tax reform has made these homes especially attractive.

If your adjusted gross income is below $100,000, you actively manage the property, and the place qualifies as a rental, you can write off up to $25,000 of any tax losses from the rental against active income (your salary) and against portfolio income (dividends and interest). But mortgage interest linked to your personal use of the property will be considered consumer interest—only partially deductible for 1990.

On the other hand, if it's a personal residence and only your second home, you may qualify for deducting your home mortgage payments and property taxes—providing the mortgages on two houses aren't for more than $100,000 plus your "acquisition indebtedness" (your original mortgages plus the cost of improvements). There's a limit on mortgage interest you can deduct if you obtained the mortgages after October 13, 1987: You can't deduct interest on a debt of over $1 million. (The $100,000 is extra.)

But if yours is a personal and not rental residence, you can deduct expenses connected with any rental period only up to the amount of your rental income. (Any excess losses can be carried forward to a time when you have excess rental income or you sell the place.)

If your vacation home doesn't qualify as your second home, your interest is considered consumer interest, only 10 percent deductible in 1990.

Remembering, too, that if you rent out the home for fewer than fifteen days you need not declare the rental income—though you won't be able to deduct any rental expenses, either. (The IRS wants to eliminate the red tape involved.) So, if your vacation home is in a resort area or an area that has a popular event once a year, seriously think of renting it for fourteen days. You can still deduct interest, taxes, and casualty/theft losses for those fourteen days.

How do you determine whether your vacation home is a rental or a personal residence, if you can use it as both?

If you yourself use the home for (a) more than fourteen days, or (b) more than 10 percent of the rental time, whichever is longer, it's a personal residence. Your deductions for maintenance and depreciation for the rental period are limited to the rental income, minus property taxes and interest for the rental period.

The IRS calculates the maintenance and depreciation expenses for the rental period by taking the same percentages of these expenses as the rental period is to the total time of use by the owner and by the renter. The IRS measures the amount of property taxes and interest, which reduce rental income, the same way.

But tax courts disagree with the IRS on how to calculate the property taxes and interest that reduce the rental income. The courts divvy up the taxes and interest in proportion to the entire year rather than in proportion to the total period of use.

Generally, you're better off using the tax court's formula when your vacation home qualifies as a personal residence, you itemize deductions, and you are under the $1 million limitation; you're better off using the IRS method when your vacation home qualifies as a rental property, and you can deduct your losses using the special $25,000 rule mentioned above.

305 DECIDE WHICH IS BETTER— RENTAL PROPERTY OR PERSONAL PROPERTY.

The answer depends in part on how much you want to use the property for yourself. As mentioned, it's a personal residence if you use it for more than fourteen days of the year—or more than 10 percent of the number of days the vacation home is rented, if that's a higher number. So, if you rent the home for 300 days, you could live there thirty days—and it still wouldn't be considered a personal residence, because you didn't exceed the 10 percent limit. You could deduct rental expenses up to your rental income, and more if you qualify for the $25,000 exception.

Your answer will also depend, in large part, on whether your adjusted gross income is over $100,000–$150,000. If that's the case, you won't be able to deduct all your tax losses. You may be wiser to use your second home as a personal residence, so as to be able to deduct all the mortgage interest (subject to the $1.1 million limitation).

If your adjusted gross income is below $100,000, and you actively manage the place, you may prefer to use the tax deductions to lower your active and portfolio income. In that case, don't spend more than fourteen days there—or more than 10 percent of the days you rent out the home. The mortgage interest for the time you spend in the home would be fully deductible, up to the purchase price of the home plus improvements.

306 DON'T COUNT MAINTENANCE DAYS AS PERSONAL DAYS.

Any days you spend working on your summer home aren't considered personal days, and thus don't reduce your fourteen-day limit. They don't count as rental days, either.

If your tenants invite you to spend a few days at your own rental house, the day or two remain rental days.

⦂ (7 DEDUCT CASUALTY LOSSES IN FULL.

With rental property, casualty and theft losses aren't subject to the $100 reduction and the reduction of 10 percent of your adjusted gross income.

⦂ 08 BE CAREFUL WHAT YOU WRITE IN YOUR LEASE.

If you require a tenant to restore your property to the exact condition in which he or she received it, you may not be entitled to depreciation. Write in your lease that the premises must be restored to their original condition, "subject to ordinary wear and tear."

⦂ (9 DON'T REPORT A SECURITY DEPOSIT AS INCOME . . .

if you accepted the deposit strictly to protect yourself against damage the tenants might cause. It would become income only if you use it and don't return it. And if you used it for repairs, you could deduct the repair expenses, up to the amount of the security deposit you used. To ensure that the deposit isn't considered advance income, have your lease call for a deposit equal to one or more month's rent, not *in lieu* of the final month's rent.

If you must pay interest to the tenant on the security deposit, it's usually not considered advance income.

⦂ 10 MAKE THE TENANT LIABLE FOR ANY PENALTY.

Let's say that your tenant sublets and breaks the law, and you must pay the penalty meted out by the courts. The tenant reimburses you, but you must declare that payment as income—and you cannot deduct the penalty.

To get around this, your lease should hold the tenant directly responsible for any penalties.

311 DON'T DECLARE ANY IMPROVEMENTS YOUR TENANT MADE.

If your tenant left them don't declare them as income. They aren't taxable to you—providing that they weren't a substitute for rent the tenant owed.

312 BOOST THE BASIS OF YOUR RAW LAND.

You can choose to add any interest and taxes you pay to the land's basis (total investment), if you don't itemize. They'll lower your taxable profits when you sell. Attach a statement to your return indicating which costs are being added to your basis.

313 CONSIDER INVESTING IN LOW-INCOME HOUSING.

If you qualify, you can get tax credits for providing housing for people with low incomes, and these credits can offset active as well as portfolio income. For new construction and for rehabilitation of buildings, a credit is available at a rate of about 9 percent of your qualifying expenses, provided the project isn't financed with tax-exempt bonds and isn't government-subsidized; for acquiring an existing building, the credit is about 4 percent. The credits are available for ten years. The credit can be used only by people earning no more than $200,000 to $250,000 a year, and by corporations. The credit can be applied against taxes due on up to $25,000 of total personal income, or $7,000 a year for those in the 28 percent bracket. You lose a $1 deduction for every $2 your income goes from $200,000 to $250,000.

Warning: Such investments are not only not liquid, but risky.

314 CONSIDER FIXING UP OLD OR HISTORIC BUILDINGS.

Again, you can get credits to offset other income—active as well as portfolio. If the building is historic—listed in the National Register of Historic Landmarks, a list of properties designated as historic by the Department of the Interior—and your rehabilitative work meets with the Department of the Interior's approval, your credit is 20 percent of eligible costs. (Property also may qualify if it's in an area certified by your state as an historic district.)

After the work is done, you cannot live in the property yourself if you want a tax credit; you must rent it out or use it as your place of business.

If it's an ordinary old building, put in use before 1936, your credit is 10 percent of your rehabilitative costs. While historic buildings can be residential or commercial for you to qualify for the credit, the ordinary old buildings must be nonresidential. As with historic property, you cannot live in the property and be entitled to the credit.

315 CONSIDER REITS.

Real Estate Investment Trusts may be the cheapest way to invest in real estate. You can buy shares of those traded on stock exchanges.

Like mutual funds, REITs invest in a variety of real-estate

ventures—from mortgages to properties. Most are traded on stock exchanges, so you have liquidity. And if they pass along most of their profits to shareholders, REITs generally don't pay much if any Federal taxes—so there's more money for *you*.

REITs that invest in properties generally have more potential for capital gains; those that invest in mortgages generally pay higher dividends.

In recent years REITs have been faring poorly, though they pay high dividends.

316 CONSIDER REMICS.

Real Estate Mortgage Investment Conduits pay competitive interest rates, and their income isn't taxed twice—first as it's received, and then as you the shareholder receive it. Only you, the shareholder, will normally be taxed on the income. That's one reason why the yield should be high. Your income, by the way, will be passive income—the kind that can be offset by tax losses from your other real estate or limited partnerships.

317 CONSIDER LIMITED PARTNERSHIPS.

Many partnerships have been restructured to emphasize income, not deductions. And these days, many partnerships are offering a degree of liquidity, with firms arranging to buy out investors' shares. Even so, these partnerships are mainly for long-term investors. One reason is that fees and commissions are high.

But many smart investors prefer REITs to limited partnerships because they are easier to evaluate.

318 CHECK UNUSED LOSSES ON LPS.

If you sold any of your passive investments, like a limited partnership, in 1989, check your 1988 return for losses on that investment that you weren't able to deduct. You can deduct them this year. In fact, if you had passive gains in 1989, you can offset them with unused losses from 1988 that you can carry forward. (If you made a passive investment before October 23, 1986, you could deduct only 65 percent of the losses in 1987 if you had no passive *income*. If you made the investment after that date, none of the loss was allowed in 1988 except against passive income.)

Chapter Eleven
HOMEOWNERS

Keep in mind that the rules for home-equity loans—second mortgages, second deeds of trust, revolving lines of credit—have been changed radically.

Now, if you bought a home or refinanced after October 13, 1987, you can—mercifully—forget all about using the proceeds for education or medical expenses in order to make all the interest you pay deductible.

What counts is that your home-equity loans not exceed $100,000 (but see Tip 322), and that your total mortgages not exceed your homes' fair market value. The $100,000 can be spent on anything at all.

Besides the home-equity limit of $100,000, you can continue to deduct your "acquisition indebtedness"—the debt you incurred in buying, building, or substantially improving your first and second homes. If you refinance your mortgage, all you can deduct is the amount outstanding before you refinanced—plus $100,000. Incidentally, if you're married and file separately, the $100,000 ceiling drops to $50,000 apiece.

There's also a new ceiling of $1 million on the deductibility of mortgage loans to buy a house, or make major improvements.

These new rules, enacted in late 1987, apply only to mortgages in place after October 13, 1987.

Example: You bought a house in 1985 for $200,000, taking out a mortgage for $160,000. The house is now worth $310,000. You also took out a $150,000 revolving line of credit in 1986. Your total mortgage debt: $160,000 plus $150,000, or $310,000. All of it is acquisition indebtedness, and all the interest on it is deductible.

But if you incurred the same debts after the 1987 change, interest on only $260,000 would be deductible. That includes interest on the $160,000 mortgage and interest on up to $100,000 of the home-equity loan.

But let's say that you won the lottery and decided to put a $1.5 million addition on your home, taking out a mortgage for the entire amount. Only interest on $690,000 of the additional $1.5 million mortgage would be deductible. Reason: The $310,000 acquisition indebtedness counts toward the $1 million limit.

Overall, the tax benefits of owning your own home, condominium, cooperative, houseboat, or whatever have been nicked by tax reform, but not grievously wounded. Homeowners still enjoy delicious deductions that renters don't—for local real-estate taxes, and (with limits) mortgage interest payments. And there are all sorts of other wonderful blessings that Uncle Sam bestows upon homeowners, just to encourage Americans to join the club. So our first piece of advice is . . .

319 BECOME A HOMEOWNER.

If a homeowner decides to borrow money to buy a car, pay a medical expense or tuition bills, or even traipse off to Tahiti, he or she may be able to deduct *all* the interest charged—by means of a home-equity loan. Renters can deduct only a shrinking percentage of such interest.

The favored fraternity of homeowners may also (1) postpone paying capital-gains taxes on their profit when they sell their houses, or perhaps never have to pay a single penny of taxes on that profit; and/or (2) shield $125,000 worth of their profit from the IRS if they meet certain rules.

In sum, if you sincerely want to be rich (or just richer), becoming a homeowner is a pretty sure way to accomplish just that.

True, the housing market is currently sluggish in many parts of the country. But the market has always been cyclical.

True, tax reform has cut back the blessings of homeownership a bit—indirectly. With tax rates down, the deductions for property taxes and for mortgage payments aren't worth as much as they used to be. If you were in the 38.5 percent tax bracket in 1987, every additional $100 you paid for any deductible expenses wound up costing you merely $61.50. (You could deduct $38.50 from your taxable income if you itemized.) In 1990, if you're in the 28 percent bracket, a deductible $100 expense will cost you $72, not just $61.50.

Then too, unless Congress changes its mind, the lenient treatment of long-term capital gains has flown out the window. (Long-term now means more than a year.) In 1986, you had to pay taxes on only 40 percent of your long-term gains. In 1987, you wouldn't have to pay more than a 28 percent rate on your gains, even if you were in the 38.5 percent bracket. In 1989 and 1990, long-term capital gains are being taxed like your salary and other "ordinary" income—perhaps as high as 33 percent. That means homeowners who can't shield their capital gains from taxes will be socked harder than they were in the past.

But deductions are better than no deductions. And those twin blessings bestowed upon homeowners—tax-deferral and the one-time $125,000 exclusion—are therefore now worth far more than ever.

Clearly, being a homeowner—before and *after* tax reform—is being on the good side of Uncle Sam.

If you're young, as a general rule, you should save up to buy a house—or a condo or coop or mobile home. If you're already a homeowner, as a general rule, remain a homeowner.

Of course, don't buy a house if you can't really afford it—if your job is insecure, or if you'll strip yourself bare of emergency money by making a down payment. And don't buy the wrong house in the wrong area. But for all sorts of reasons besides tax reasons, *do* try to buy a house.

320   BE WARY OF BUYING A HOUSE FOR ALL CASH.

The trouble is, if you buy a house, borrow money, and don't use your new house as collateral, you may not be able to deduct the interest.

321   CONSIDER FINANCING YOUR RENOVATIONS.

Acquisition debt can include "substantial improvements," but only if those improvements were financed by loans secured by the property.

322 DON'T THINK THAT $100,000 IS WRIT IN STONE.

You can deduct interest in full on more than $100,000 in home-equity loans—if you use the proceeds (a) for home improvements, (b) for investments, up to your investment income plus $2,000 (for 1989), or (c) for your business. And, of course, you can deduct 20 percent of the interest on the excess over $100,000 for 1989, and 10 percent for 1990 (unless that's eliminated entirely).

323 BUY A HOUSE THIS YEAR.

You can begin deducting your property taxes and mortgage interest *this* year if you buy a house now rather than waiting. Remember the cardinal rule of tax-avoidance: Defer income, and *take deductions now*.

You can also deduct any points you might pay to obtain your mortgage. Points are special charges lenders may levy to lower the interest rate on your mortgage. Each point equals 1 percent of your loan. If you take out a $50,000 mortgage and must pay three points, it's $1,500. You can deduct these points all at once in the year you pay them if (a) you obtain a new mortgage to buy or improve your home (you don't refinance your old one), and (b) you pay the charges up front, all at once—you don't add the charges to your mortgage balance, paying them off over the life of your loan. You must also segregate money you pay for points from other closing costs, like title insurance. Use a separate check. ("Closing" refers to transactions during the final sale of real estate.)

Of course, there may be good reasons for you *not* to buy a house this year. You might have more money for a down payment next year, and thus be able to wangle a mortgage at a lower interest rate by making a more hefty down payment. Or you want to make sure that your job is stable, or you think your local housing market is too high and prices might plummet. But other things being equal, buy a house this year rather than next.

324 CONSIDER A HOUSE IN A LOW-TAX COMMUNITY.

You can still deduct local real-estate taxes. But the deduction isn't worth as much, what with tax rates having gone down. That's why you should now pay more attention to your property taxes. If you're considering buying in one of two communities, pay more attention to the one with lower property taxes—providing that the services that the community provides (education, police, fire, sanitation) are on a par with the other community.

325 DEDUCT THE INTEREST ON A RECREATIONAL VEHICLE YOU BOUGHT ON CREDIT.

It probably qualifies as a second residence, so the interest is mortgage and not personal interest (only 20 percent deductible for 1989). The same goes for a large boat. Such "residences," adds Thomas B. Gau, a CPA and certified financial planner in Torrance, California, must have a kitchen, toilet, and sleeping facilities. "Porta Potties will do," he adds.

326 DEDUCT AS INTEREST ANY LATE-PAYMENT MORTGAGE CHARGES.

Banks don't include the charges as interest in their year-end statements.

327 CONSIDER A HOME-EQUITY LOAN.

To hear lenders tell it, the home-equity line of credit is just about the most wonderful innovation since double-entry bookkeeping. But to hear consumer advocates talk, the home-equity line of credit is more akin to the invention of debtors' prisons.

The truth lies somewhere in between. Such loans can be a blessing for the sophisticated, and—for the unsophisticated—the equivalent of a loaded pistol in the hands of a temperamental child.

Now, a home-equity line of credit is a loan backed by the value of your free-and-clear ownership (equity) in your first or second home. Typically you can borrow up to 75 percent of that equity. So, if your house is worth $100,000 and the outstanding balance on your first mortgage is $20,000, you could borrow up to $55,000 ($100,000 times 75 percent minus $20,000).

If, instead of a line of credit, you were to get a $55,000 second mortgage, you would receive a lump sum and begin paying interest on the total amount. But with a line of credit, you can borrow up to $55,000 at any time. If you withdrew $5,000, you'd pay interest only on that $5,000—and the remaining $50,000 would remain available.

Home-equity lines of credit thus cost you less: You don't pay interest except on the amount you borrow. Other advantages:

A. MUCH OF THE INTEREST YOU PAY MAY BE DEDUCTIBLE. The Tax Reform Act of 1986 started lowering the boom on interest you can deduct for "consumer" debt—for car payments, credit card loans, and so forth. You can deduct only 20 percent for 1989, 10 percent for 1990, and zilch after that.

But you can still fully deduct the interest you pay on loans secured by your first or second residences—up to $100,000. (If you obtained a mortgage before October 14, 1987, there's no limit on what's deductible.)

This means that if you were planning to borrow to pay for something expensive—a boat, a vacation trip—you can now obtain a home-equity line of credit and magically make all of *that* interest deductible.

Yet these potential tax benefits shouldn't sweep you off your feet. Reasons:

• High closing costs (for an appraisal, legal fees, and so forth) can easily wipe out any tax savings on a small home-equity line of credit.

• Tax-wise, you may be better off getting a loan a few years down the road, when consumer interest may be only 10 percent deductible—or not at all.

• Finally, with tax rates having shrunk, deductions in general aren't as valuable now.

In short, you'll have to do some figuring to make sure the tax benefits of such a loan are worthwhile.

B. THE TERMS CAN BE ATTRACTIVE. You may be able to swing a home-equity line of credit with no closing costs at all, or modest ones—$250, say, for a $20,000 loan. (Generally, 1.25 percent of the loan is standard.)

If you're paying 17 to 18 percent interest on credit cards, or 14 percent on personal loans, both of which are only partly deductible, why not pay 12 percent, fully deductible, on a home-equity line of credit?

Again, a few provisos:

• A straightforward second mortgage may be better if you need a lump sum for, say, a home improvement, and not continuing loans for, say, tuition payments. While closing costs may be higher with a second mortgage, you're more likely to wangle a fixed rate of interest which is more desirable than an adjustable rate. Lines of credit usually carry a variable rate, floating with the prime, and often with no cap, or limit, on how much the rate can rise.

• Refinancing your first mortgage may also be better. You'll probably pay a lower interest rate, get a longer term (up to thirty years, whereas a typical line of credit may come due in five or ten years), and more money as well (80 percent of a house's value should be a breeze). If your first mortgage is at a relatively high rate, you're probably *far* better off refinancing.

C. YOU MAY HAVE A GOOD REASON TO BORROW. Prudent homeowners might encounter an investment opportunity that, taken at the flood, will lead to fortune. Or they may want to launch their own well-planned businesses, send themselves to graduate school, or bring their nineteenth-century kitchens into the late twentieth century.

Now, the arguments *against* home-equity lines of credit:

A. YOU COULD LOSE YOUR HOUSE. If you default on credit card charges, Visa or MasterCard is unlikely to compel you to sell your house at public auction. Most states protect all of your home, or a percentage, against creditors. If you default on paying off a car, the bank that financed it will just take it back. But you *could* lose your home by defaulting on a line of credit loan, and that could happen if you lose your job, become ill, or separate from your spouse.

"Your house doesn't make the payments," notes Robert J. Hobbs, staff lawyer with the National Consumer Law Center in Boston. "*You* make the payments. And if your income declines, you could be in big trouble."

B. SOME PEOPLE ABUSE THEIR LOANS. Most Americans, if they were to obtain such loans, would do it to consolidate their debts, according to a Harris poll. This seems to be a worthy purpose. But if people have gone haywire with charge accounts and credit cards, it's not improbable that they will go haywire with home-equity lines of credit, particularly the kind that come with credit cards.

Getting too much money too soon is dangerous enough. It's even worse when it's "funny money." There's less pain in writing a check than paying cash, less pain in using a credit card than writing a check.

The fundamental danger is that homeowners will not recognize the wisdom of letting the money supposedly "locked" in their homes just sit there quietly appreciating— instead of threatening it by means of an ill-considered loan.

Few investments are as solid as real estate. It appreciates nicely in normal times, spectacularly in inflationary times. Your equity in your home also serves as a cushion against emergencies. If you pay off your mortgage, you can probably afford to remain in your old homestead when you retire, or you can trade down to a smaller house in the area, using your profit to bolster your retirement funds.

But you may not be able to retire *when* you want to, or *where* you want to, if you're still paying off mortgages or if you have scant equity in your home.

To find the best home-equity loan available, look for

- no fees of any kind—no closing costs and no bank charges
- a fixed rate of interest (You'll know what to expect from month to month.)
- next best, a variable interest rate, but with caps on how high the rate can go, and how fast
- a requirement that the borrower immediately begin repaying principal (Otherwise, you may stall and stall—and owe more and more.)

• no prepayment penalty (If you don't have a fixed-rate loan, you may want to pay off the balance if interest rates suddenly rise—and you won't want to be hit by an extra charge.)

• no ongoing fees—such as charges for checks, or a penalty for not using the credit that's available, or fees for "general administration"

If your lender doesn't offer a credit card attached to the home-equity loan, it may be a sign that the lender is responsible, and doesn't want borrowers using the money for frivolous reasons.

328 GET ONE ONLY FOR A SPECIFIC PURPOSE.

A man in Massachusetts went from prosperity almost to the poorhouse thanks to home-equity loans. He used them as a giant credit card; when his income suddenly slid, he got into serious trouble. He has this advice for others interested in such loans: "Get one for a specific purpose, and use it only for that specific purpose. Don't let it lull you into a false sense of unlimited wealth."

329 REMAIN IN A HOME YOU OWN.

Once you leave, for an apartment or another residence you don't own, you may owe taxes on any profits you've made from selling your home. So, apart from the fact that most people prefer living in their own homes, for tax reasons try to live in residences that you yourself own. And try not to move often. If you move every few years, closing costs will cut down if not cancel out your gains.

When you and your spouse die, your heirs will inherit the house without ever having to pay any taxes on the capital gains your house (or houses) have garnered over the years. (Death may be inevitable, but obviously that's not always true of taxes.) The other two chief ways of reducing or eliminating capital-gains taxes on the sale of your residence follow.

330 ROLL OVER YOUR GAINS.

You can postpone (at least) paying taxes on the appreciation of your house when you sell it if

a. you buy and live in another main home within two years after (or before) selling your old one. Yes, you can qualify even if you buy (or build) a new main home two years before selling your old one.

b. the new home is as expensive as or more expensive than the old one.

c. the homes you sold and bought are your main residences (not your summer homes). You could, of course, buy a second home in a resort area, use it as a vacation home for two years, *then* make it your main residence when you sell your other home.

You can use this deferral tactic over and over. But you cannot use it more than once every two years—unless you move because of a job change and you fulfill the requirements to deduct the expenses on your tax return if you itemized your deductions.

The postponement of these taxes could come back to haunt you, though. The basis of (total investment in) your *new* house is lowered by whatever amount you avoided paying taxes on. If you avoided paying taxes on $20,000 of capital gains, then bought a $100,000 house, its basis would be only $80,000. That means that someday—when you sell that $100,000 house—you might have to pay taxes on that $20,000 profit. But you may be in a lower tax bracket when that day comes—and you'll have had all that extra time to use the money as you see fit. But remember: If you die while owning that residence, the IRS will ignore all those capital gains.

What if you don't need a bigger house? How can you still buy a house at least as expensive and thus defer paying taxes on your gain? Buy a smaller house—but in a more expensive area. Or add improvements within two years of selling your old house, to bring the cost of your new house up to the sales price of your old one. Many people sell their homes when their kids move out, and buy a smaller place— but with larger grounds, just to have a more expensive house for tax purposes.

If your main house is a trailer, houseboat, or yacht, it still qualifies for the deferral tactic—whether it's your old or your new residence. And your replacement residence doesn't even have to be in this country. In fact, if your home is outside the country—because, say, you're in the armed forces—you may have longer than two years to buy or build a replacement home.

331 ROLL OVER YOUR GAINS—EVEN IF YOUR FIANCÉ IS.

You're selling a residence and rolling over the gains. You can do this even if you bought a new residence with your fiancé, and he is *also* rolling over the gains from selling a residence. If the new residence is as expensive as the total of the two places that you and your fiancé sold, or more expensive, you can defer all capital-gains taxes. (The two of you must attach a statement to your tax returns consenting to this rollover.)

332 SELL YOUR OLD RESIDENCE TO YOUR CORPORATION . . .

if you're having trouble selling it and you're close to the twenty-four-month period during which you can defer gains by buying a new residence. If you have an incorporated business, sell your old house (at fair market value) to your business. This will qualify you to defer paying taxes on the gain. When your corporation sells the property, it may have to pay taxes on some ordinary income.

333 CHOOSE WHICH GAIN TO PAY TAXES ON.

You may have a choice. Let's say that you sell your house for $100,000. You have a $20,000 gain. You buy another house for $92,000. Do you owe taxes on the $20,000 gain—or on the $8,000 that cannot be deferred? The IRS lets you choose the lower amount—in this case, the $8,000 that cannot be deferred. The other $12,000 is subtracted from the $92,000 to become the tax basis of your new house—$78,000.

334 BOOST YOUR HOUSE'S BASIS.

The higher your house's basis, the less capital gains there will be that might be taxed—if you ever are required to pay those taxes. Here's what you can add to your purchase price:

• closing costs, such as legal fees, recorder's fees, title insurance, and a termite inspection.

• the cost of improvements. Examples are a new furnace, new carpeting, a new fence, central air-conditioning, new wiring or new plumbing. Repairs—such as patching your roof, or having a leaky pipe fixed—don't qualify. You can use the original cost of your improvements—even if you tacked down that carpeting years ago and it's rather tacky now. Don't count your own labor as part of the cost of an improvement. (This is a good argument for letting someone else do it.)

• legal expenses connected with any improvements—such as your hiring a lawyer to get a variance (an exception to the planning code) so you can add an extra room.

• a real-estate agent's fee, if you as a buyer used an agent (which seems to be growing more common).

• the cost of appliances and other items you bought and left with the purchaser of your house, so long as you didn't sell them separately from the house (room air conditioners, stove, microwave, and so forth).

• assessments for local improvements, like new sidewalks or the widening of streets.

By the same token, you must lower your basis by casualty losses that you deducted in previous years (like the cost of a living room that was destroyed by fire); by residential energy credits you took (remember them?); and, of course, by any gains deferred from sales of your other houses.

335 DON'T FORGET ANY IMPROVEMENTS.

You won't overlook major items like an addition to your house, a new deck, or central air-conditioning. But don't forget new shelves, a repaved or widened driveway, new plants and bushes, wallpapering a room that had been painted. Inspect your property, inside and outside, to refresh your memory. And don't forget very small improvements. Examples: new locks, doorbells, a security system, termite-proofing, smoke detectors that go with the house, a lawn-sprinkler system.

336 ADD TO YOUR BASIS EVEN IF YOU DON'T HAVE RECEIPTS.

Ideally, you'll have kept all your canceled checks, credit-card chits, and sales slips. If not, you may be able to get away with building permits for improvements, property-tax records, or before-and-after photographs of your house.

337 CONSIDER A HOME-IMPROVEMENT LOAN.

If you obtain such a loan, backed by your equity in your house, you can deduct the interest, in full. The best bets, as far as getting a good return on your investment: a good new kitchen; anything that brings your house up to the level of houses around you—for example, adding a third bedroom if houses around you have three or more; and remedying any defects your house has—not enough bathrooms, for instance. Such improvements should add a good chunk to the value of your house. And if you must someday pay a capital-gains tax on the house's profits, you can add the cost of your improvements to the house price, thus reducing your tax. Meanwhile, of course, your house will have been more pleasurable to live in.

You can deduct points you paid for a home-improvement loan, this year, provided that the loan was secured by your house.

338 REFINANCE YOUR MORTGAGE.

As a rule, if current mortgage interest rates are two percentage points below the rate you're paying now, and you plan on living in your home for at least a few years, it's probably worthwhile to get a new mortgage. First of all, you'll save on mortgage payments. And, second, assuming you refinance for more than your current mortgage balance, you will have more money at your disposal (because you will have paid off some of the principal). And the interest on the amount of your new mortgage may be fully deductible, provided that it's less than your acquisition indebtedness plus $100,000.

But the two-percentage point rule is only rough. The longer you plan to continue living in your home, the less the spread can be between your current mortgage interest rate and what you can refinance for. But even a one-percentage point spread can save you money if you remain in your house for four or five years.

339 DEDUCT POINTS YEAR-BY-YEAR . . .

if you refinanced your mortgage or bought a dwelling that you'll rent out. If you paid $3,000 in points for a thirty-year mortgage, you can deduct $100 a year.

When you sell your house—or just pay off your mortgage—you can deduct all the remaining points.

340 HAVE POINTS ADDED TO YOUR MORTGAGE BALANCE . . .

assuming that you've refinanced your mortgage, or bought a dwelling to rent it out. You're charged points, which you can deduct only over the life of the mortgage. Try to pay the points over the life of the mortgage. That way, you'll spare yourself some calculations.

341 REDUCE YOUR GAIN WITH MOVING EXPENSES YOU COULDN'T DEDUCT.

You're better off itemizing your moving expenses, to get your deductions sooner. (See Chapter 4.) But if you don't itemize (because the sum of your deductions doesn't exceed the standard deduction), or you've reached the limits on your deductible moving expenses, add whatever expenses you can to the basis of your house or to the adjusted sales price. For example, reduce the basis of your new home by a real-estate agent's commission you paid.

342 LOWER YOUR TAXABLE SALES PRICE.

By lowering your sales price for tax purposes, your gain will again be lower. Here's what you can subtract to wind up with your "adjusted sales price":

- real-estate agent's commissions
- legal fees, geological surveys, maps, termite inspections, and so forth
- any loan charges, such as points, that you as the seller must pay (if your buyer obtained, for example, a Veterans Administration-backed mortgage)
- the cost of advertising, for-sale signs, and fact sheets if you sold your house yourself, without benefit of a broker. (You can deduct them even if you wound up having a broker sell your house.)
- fix-up expenses for work performed during the ninety days before you sold your home, and paid for within thirty days after the sale (The narrow time-limit is to ensure that the expenses were truly to help you sell the house.) Examples: the cost of having the exterior or interior of your house painted, your plumbing repaired, new wallpaper installed. You can deduct fix-up costs only if you buy a less expensive house—because if you buy a house as expensive, you must defer the gains. The fix-up costs would then serve to boost the basis of your new house.

Here's an example of all these calculations, provided by the IRS:

Your selling expenses were $5,000. You spent $900 on

new blinds and on a new water heater; you also spent $800 on painting your house—and met the rules regarding such fix-up expenses.

1. Selling price of old home: $61,400
2. Selling expenses: $5,000
3. Amount realized (1 minus 2): $56,400
4. Basis of old home: $45,000
5. Improvements (blinds, heater): $900
6. New basis of home (4 plus 5): $45,900
7. Gain on old home (3 minus 6): $10,500

You buy and live in another home costing $54,600 within two years of selling your old one. Now you can defer paying taxes on most of that $10,500.

8. Amount realized: $56,400
9. Fix-up expenses (painting): $800
10. Adjusted sales price (8 minus 9): $55,600
11. Cost of replacement home: $54,600
12. Gain *not* postponed (10 minus 11): $1,000
13. Gain postponed (7 minus 12): $9,500
14. Cost of new home: $54,600
15. Adjusted basis of new home (14 minus 13): $45,100

343 DEDUCT A LOSS ON SELLING YOUR HOUSE . . .

if you were renting it out. Some homeowners who are selling for losses—typically because they bought a home in a deteriorating neighborhood, or where the main industry left—rent their houses for a few months, then try to deduct their loss. No good. You must prove to the IRS that you were renting the house for a profit, not just to deduct the loss on its sale. The longer you were renting it out, the more persuasive a case you can make. And you may need appraisals showing that the house had *not* declined in value before you began renting it out.

344 TAKE THE $125,000 EXCLUSION.

You can subtract $125,000 from your gain if (a) your house was your main residence, (b) you or your spouse were fifty-five when you sold the house (you didn't turn fifty-five at the end of that year) and owned it jointly, and (c) you or your spouse lived there for three of the five years before you sold it. One person—you or your spouse—must meet all three rules.

You can use this exclusion just once in your lifetime. But you can undo a mistake. Let's say that you use the exclusion to escape taxes on $20,000 of gain. You buy another house, and a few years later, you sell that one, for a $50,000 gain. You have three years from the date that your earlier return (with the smaller $20,000 exclusion) was due to be filed to cancel that first exclusion.

345 TAKE THE EXCLUSION EVEN IF YOUR QUALIFYING SPOUSE DIED.

If you and your spouse owned the house jointly, and your spouse was fifty-five or older, and had lived there for three of the past five years, you qualify for the exclusion—even if you're not fifty-five, or hadn't lived in the house for three of the past five years.

346 CONSIDER THE EXCLUSION WHEN YOU MARRY.

Let's say you've never used the exclusion, and you're living in your own house. Now you plan to marry someone who *has* used the exclusion before, and you plan to live in your house when you marry. You'll be better off selling your house before you marry. The fact that your new spouse has used the $125,000 exclusion would keep *you* from being able to use it—or even half of it!

▪ 47 TAKE THE EXCLUSION IF YOU'RE DIVORCED ...

even if your ex-spouse had claimed the exclusion before marrying you. This would hold true also if your spouse had died and had used it before marrying you.

▪ 48 TAKE THE EXCLUSION EVEN IF YOU RENTED OUT THE HOUSE.

You qualify if you rented the house for two years, and lived there the previous three years.

▪ 49 TAKE THE EXCLUSION IF YOU WERE IN A NURSING HOME ...

and you didn't live in the house for three of the past five years. But you must have lived there for a total of one year during that time. You must have been physically or mentally incapable of self-care, and the care must have been given in a state licensed facility.

▪ 50 CHOOSE DEFERRAL OVER THE EXCLUSION.

By and large, the deferral tactic is better. You can use it again and again. And at a later time in your life, the exclusion may be more suitable—because you may want to live in a small house, or in an apartment. Also, your taxable gain may be higher later in life, because of the lowered basis of your last house, the result of all those deferrals.

351 TAKE BOTH.

Consider taking all of the $125,000 exclusion, *and* deferring the tax you owe on your remaining profit.

Here's an example, from the accounting firm of Seidman & Seidman/BDO:

You're fifty-five, and sell your primary residence for $400,000. The basis of your residence was $75,000.

1. Sales price of old home: $400,000
2. Tax basis of old home: $75,000
3. Gain (1 minus 2): $325,000
4. Exclusion: $125,000
5. Taxable gain (3 minus 4): $200,000

Now let's say that you buy a new house for $300,000. And now you can invoke the deferral tactic—even though your new house costs far less than your old one!

6. Sales price: $400,000
7. Exclusion: $125,000
8. New sales price (6 minus 7): $275,000
9. Price of new home: $300,000
10. Taxable gain (8 minus 9): 0
11. Tax basis of new home (9 minus 5): $100,000

352 OWN YOUR HOUSE JOINTLY.

That way, if you or your spouse die, the surviving spouse will inherit the house without court probate costs.

353 SELL YOUR HOUSE TO YOUR KIDS.

If you're getting on in years and need the money, sell your house to your children, in return for an annuity—a regular stream of payments for as long as you live. Otherwise, your house will be subject to estate taxes when you die, and your children's inheritance will shrink.

Chapter Twelve
EMPLOYEES

Tax reform has curtailed many deductions for employees. Now, many of their job-related expenses must be listed on Schedule A as "miscellaneous" expenses, instead of being deducted directly from gross income. And their total job-related expenses (together with other miscellaneous deductions) must exceed 2 percent of their adjusted gross incomes before they can be used as itemized deductions. (Adjusted gross income: total income minus things like alimony you pay.)

Still, there are steps you can take to keep your tax bill down, beginning with

354 DEDUCT FOR REIMBURSED BUSINESS EXPENSES.

Check your W-2 form. Did you receive reimbursements for business expenses, like a car allowance, that are included as income? If you did, you can deduct those reimbursements in full as an adjustment to your income on the first page of Form 1040. Report your expenses on Form 2106.

355 ASK YOUR EMPLOYER TO PAY LAST YEAR'S (AND FUTURE) BUSINESS ENTERTAINMENT EXPENSES.

Reason: to deduct them yourself, you must itemize, and all your miscellaneous expenses must surpass 2 percent of your adjusted gross income. Even then, you'll lose 20 percent of all such expenses—because only 80 percent of entertainment expenses are now deductible.

If you offer to take a retroactive salary cut for last year, equal to your entertainment expenses, your employer may be more amenable.

356 ASK YOUR BOSS TO PAY YOUR CAR EXPENSES . . .

instead of your getting an allowance for the use of your car (which you must declare). Again, all your expenses may not be deductible because of the 2 percent floor. Or ask your employer to provide you with a car.

357 HAVE YOUR EMPLOYER PAY MORE OF YOUR MEDICAL EXPENSES.

Your out-of-pocket expenses are unlikely to exceed 7.5 percent of your adjusted gross income. Again, offer to take a salary cut in exchange for more comprehensive medical coverage.

■ 58 PUSH YOUR EMPLOYEE-RELATED EXPENSES INTO ONE YEAR.

That way, your expenses may exceed the 2 percent floor.

■ 59 DON'T FORGET BUSINESS PHONE CALLS FROM YOUR HOME ...

if your employer didn't reimburse you. And deduct the cost of call-waiting if it's for a business phone in your home. You can also deduct the cost of installing a business phone. But after 1988, you are not entitled to deduct the basic monthly cost of the first phone in your residence.

■ 60 DON'T FORGET SUBSCRIPTIONS TO BUSINESS PUBLICATIONS.

Those relating to your occupation will qualify.

■ 61 DON'T FORGET JOB-HUNTING EXPENSES ...

in your same line of work, even if you don't get an offer or you turn the job down.

■ 62 DON'T FORGET EDUCATIONAL EXPENSES ...

providing they don't qualify you for a new career. But they can help you keep your job, salary, or status, or improve or maintain the skills you need in your job.

Educational expenses include tuition, books, supplies, lab fees, and hiring a researcher or typist to help you prepare a paper—as well as transportation, lodging, and meal expenses in certain circumstances.

Usually you must attach Form 2106, "Employee Business Expenses." If you're self-employed, fill out the appropriate lines on Schedule C.

363 DEDUCT TRAVEL EXPENSES FOR STUDY OR RESEARCH.

If you travel for a specific purpose, you may still be able to deduct your expenses—if your employer doesn't cover the cost. Example: You take a course not available elsewhere. You must subtract 20 percent of the cost of meals and entertainment.

364 INCLUDE TRANSPORTATION COSTS.

If your educational courses are deductible, so are the transportation costs to and fro. You can deduct for taxis, trains, buses, or the use of your own car (at 24 cents a mile for the first 15,000 miles and 11 cents a mile thereafter). Don't forget tolls and parking fees. (Check that these numbers haven't changed.)

365 DEDUCT THE COST OF TRAVEL AND LODGING.

A school teacher was allowed to deduct the cost of travel and lodgings in Alaska while he improved his job skills.

366 DEDUCT FOR SCHOOLING THAT QUALIFIES YOU FOR A PROMOTION.

A teacher can deduct the cost of courses to become a principal. A high-school or elementary-school teacher can deduct the cost of courses to become a college teacher.

⋮ 67 DEDUCT THE COST OF AN INITIAL DEGREE . . .

if your employer changes your job's requirements. Example:
The U.S. Army began requiring officers below captain to
have a bachelor's degree. Such officers could deduct the cost
of obtaining undergraduate degrees.

⋮ 68 SKIP ADVANCED COURSES UNTIL YOU GET A CREDENTIAL.

If you're becoming a lawyer, for instance, wait until you
have obtained your degree before taking an advanced course
in, say, taxes. The advanced course would be deductible
after you've become a lawyer, but not before.

⋮ 69 REMEMBER THE $5,250 EXCLUSION.

That's the amount you can receive from your employer for
educational assistance without its being considered income.
But you cannot be doing graduate work.

⋮ 70 DON'T CHANGE YOUR LISTED OCCUPATION.

If you've deducted educational courses, don't change the
occupation you've listed at the top of your tax return if your
job really hasn't changed. That might suggest to the IRS that
you've switched careers—and your educational expenses may
not have been deductible.

371 DEDUCT EDUCATIONAL EXPENSES TO PROTECT YOUR JOB.

You can deduct such expenses if you need them to keep you
from losing your current job benefits even if they don't

necessarily maintain or improve your skills in your job. A teacher deducted the cost of courses she took only to qualify for annual salary increases.

372 TAKE DEDUCTIONS IF YOU'VE LEFT YOUR JOB TEMPORARILY.

If you leave your job to study, take courses related to your work, then return to your job or a similar one, you can deduct the cost of the education. Your absence was "temporary." An absence of a year or so is normally considered temporary, but sometimes the IRS has approved longer absences.

373 DEDUCT FOR STUDYING EVEN IF YOU WORK ONLY PART-TIME.

Someone who is partly retired can deduct educational expenses that otherwise qualify.

374 DEDUCT FOR COURSES OUTSIDE A UNIVERSITY.

A correspondence school qualifies, and so do the lessons given by a private instructor.

375 DON'T FORGET DUES.

Either those you pay your union or your professional association.

376 DEDUCT FOR UNION DUES . . .

even if you're not a member, but you must belong to the union because you receive union benefits. If you would be dropped from membership unless you pay a fine, the fine would be deductible.

377 DEDUCT PART OF THE DUES FOR COUNTRY CLUBS . . .

if you use them more than 50 percent of the time to help you in your business. But you can deduct only the portion of your dues directly related to your business.

378 DON'T FORGET TO DEDUCT 80 PERCENT OF ENTERTAINMENT EXPENSES.

Example: taking a client to dinner and discussing business.

379 HAVE A GOOD EXCUSE FOR EXPENSIVE MEALS.

If you take someone out for an expensive meal, be prepared to explain that the person was an important client, about to throw a lot of business your way. The IRS won't allow deductions for "lavish and extravagant" meals.

380 KEEP GOOD RECORDS FOR ENTERTAINMENT EXPENSES.

The old rule: You must record the time, place, and the cost of the entertainment and meals, and the name of the person you entertained. Now you must also record the specific business transacted, or the topic of business conversation that took place during the meal.

⁞ 81 CONSIDER DEDUCTING THEATER TICKETS AS "ENTERTAINMENT."

You give theater tickets to a business associate. As a gift, your deduction would be limited to $25 per person. You may be better listing it as an entertainment expense, which has no limits. But remember that entertainment expenses have a 20 percent bite taken out before they're deductible.

⁞ 82 DEDUCT YOUR SPOUSE'S EXPENSES . . .

if you entertain a business customer, and his or her spouse joins you. It's an "ordinary and necessary" business expense because it would be awkward if your spouse didn't join you.

⁞ 83 DON'T FORGET LEGAL EXPENSES.

They must be job connected—like paying a lawyer to help you negotiate an employment contract.

⁞ 84 DON'T FORGET PERIODIC HEALTH EXAMS YOUR EMPLOYER REQUIRES.

Assuming, of course, you aren't reimbursed.

385 DON'T SUBTRACT 2 PERCENT FROM ALL DEDUCTIONS.

Moving expenses, for example, aren't subject to the new ceiling you must surpass. Other itemized deductions that bypass the new 2 percent rule:

• the special work expenses of a handicapped person relating to the impairment (typically, paying an attendant to help you on the job and the cost of special tools)

• employment expenses of certain performing artists—those who work for at least two employers in the performing arts during the year (with at least $200 in earnings from each), whose expenses exceed 10 percent of their gross wages, and whose adjusted gross incomes (before these expenses) are not over $16,000.

: 86 DON'T LIST CERTAIN EMPLOYEE EXPENSES UNDER "MISCELLANEOUS."

Certain employee expenses still qualify as adjustments to income—you needn't itemize to benefit from them. Among them: reimbursed employee expenses (they're balanced out by your reporting the reimbursement as income).

: 87 DON'T FORGET ANY MISCELLANEOUS DEDUCTIONS.

Such as malpractice or errors and omissions insurance, employment-agency and career-counseling fees, and a college professor's lecturing and writing expenses.

: 88 DON'T FORGET TO DEDUCT THE COST OF WORK CLOTHES

They must be required for your job and must be clothes you wouldn't wear off the job.

: 89 DEDUCT FOR HAVING WORK CLOTHES CLEANED . . .

if it's a question of safety (you work around machinery, and baggy clothing might get entangled). Those who can deduct the cost of work clothes include athletes, firefighters, police officers, letter carriers, nurses, civilian teachers in a military school. A painter deducted white overalls his employer required; surgeons can deduct surgical smocks; a car repairman deducted high-top shoes, jumpers, and leather-palm gloves, an art teacher deducted the cost of protective smocks.

⁝ 90 DON'T DEDUCT THE COST OF YOUR BRIEFCASE.

IRS agents probably don't deduct the cost of *their* brief-cases. Why tick them off?

⁝ 91 DON'T OVERLOOK ANY SMALL TRAVEL EXPENSES . . .

such as the cost of dry cleaning and laundry, tips, phone calls home, as well as transportation, food, and lodgings.

Travel expenses are defined as those you incur outside the metropolitan area where you work, and if you remain overnight—or at least long enough to need some rest before you return.

⁝ 92 USE THE COST OF A SINGLE ROOM . . .

if you took your spouse along on a business trip. Don't deduct half the cost of a double room. A single might cost $100, a double $120. Go for $100, not for half of $120.

⁝ 93 DEDUCT COMMUTING COSTS . . .

if you must travel between one place to another for the same employer, or for different employers. You can deduct only the cost of going from one place to another—not the cost of leaving and returning home. Normal commuting costs are not deductible.

394 DEDUCT OTHER COMMUTING COSTS UNDER SPECIAL CIRCUMSTANCES.

Two police officers who used their own cars to drive to and from work were allowed to deduct maintenance and operational expenses between their residences and police headquarters. They were officially on duty during that time— they weren't commuting.

395 DEDUCT FOR THE COST OF SITUATION-WANTED ADS.

Other job-hunting expenses you might overlook: phone calls to set up interviews, photocopying of documents like articles you've written or presentations you've made, photographs that accompany your résumés, stamps and envelopes to mail out résumés, and transportation to potential employers and to employment agencies.

396 DEDUCT THE COST OF A REWARD . . .

if you lost a briefcase or other valuable business property and you paid for the advertisement and the reward.

397 DON'T DEDUCT JUST TWENTY-FOUR CENTS A MILE IF YOU USE YOUR CAR.

You're probably better off keeping a record of your actual expenses for oil and gas, parking fees, repairs, insurance, and tolls.

398 DEDUCT FOR A HOME COMPUTER.

You may be able to use the Section 179 ("expensing") deduction to write off the cost of a computer—up to $10,000—in one year. For a full write-off, you must be able to prove that the computer was used entirely for business. For a partial deduction, you must generally use the computer more than 50 percent of the time for business. The time you use your computer for investments can be deducted, but it doesn't count toward the more-than-50 percent rule.

You cannot expense a computer's cost if you don't use it more than 50 percent of the time for business. You must depreciate a portion of the cost, using the straight-line depreciation.

399 DECIDE WHICH IS BETTER— ACTUAL CAR EXPENSES OR THE STANDARD RATE.

You can either deduct actual expenses or deduct a standard mileage rate. The second has the advantage of less record keeping. But use Form 2106, to work it out both ways, and see which saves you more money. Studies have indicated that the actual cost to operate a car may be over twice the current per-mile allowance.

The standard-mileage rate: Deduct 24 cents a mile for the first 15,000 miles of business use, 11 cents a mile above that.

400 DON'T JUST USE THE STANDARD-MILEAGE RATE.

Also deduct parking fees and tolls.

401 DEPRECIATE YOUR CAR.

A car put into business use must be depreciated over six years. During the first year, you cannot deduct more than $2,560 of the cost, $4,100 in year two, $2,450 in year three, and $1,475 in each of the next three years. Reduce the depreciation by the percentage of your personal use of the car.

If your business use of the car is 50 percent or less, you must use straight-line depreciation. And you cannot expense the cost.

402 USE A NEWER CAR FOR BUSINESS.

If you have a choice of cars, consider using the one with less than 60,000 business miles on it. That way you can deduct 24 cents a mile, up to 15,000 miles a year, instead of the 11-cents-a-mile rate required for cars already driven for 60,000 business miles or more.

403 KEEP YOUR "LUXURY" CAR FOR PERSONAL USE.

A luxury car is one that costs $12,800 or more, so it takes more years to write it off. You can depreciate a less expensive car faster. So visit customers in your Hyundai and drive to the shore in your Mercedes.

Chapter Thirteen
ENTREPRENEURS

One important recent change that employers should keep in mind: Beginning in 1988, you must pay Social Security taxes on your spouse or child (eighteen or over) if they work for you. This is the case if you run an unincorporated trade or business.

Tax reform cut back on many other tax breaks for business people. Of course, there's the famous 20 percent subtraction of expenses for meals and entertainment (the "three-martini lunch"). And the "quiet" meal—social chitchat with a customer—won't cut it anymore; you must talk about specific business matters to get a deduction. Meanwhile, depreciation periods have generally been lengthened. (For more on writing off computers, and using cars for business, see the previous chapter.)

Even so, business owners still enjoy many breaks, which is why our first suggestion is that you

404 START YOUR OWN BUSINESS.

If you have a sideline activity—photography, painting, golfing—consider making it a business. If your motive is profit, that's all you need to deduct any losses. You don't actually have to *make* a profit. But in order to deduct losses, you must run the business as if it were a business, intending to make a profit. Use a separate checking account for business receipts and disbursements, keep books showing income and expenses, have business cards printed.

Recently the Tax Court allowed a high-school teacher in Chicago to write off the cost of his golfing, including his trips to Florida. Yet his expenses exceeded his income for five consecutive years! On the other hand, his income had been steadily increasing, and he had kept meticulous records.

405 CLAIM A HOME OFFICE.

You can deduct the expenses of a home office—if you're self-employed or if you're an employee and the office is for the convenience of your employer—even if the employer doesn't require it. The rules are strict, but if you qualify, you can save a sizable amount of taxes. It's much easier to qualify if you're self-employed, or are running a sideline business.

Rules: Your office at home must be used as (a) your main place of business (it can be a sideline business), or (b) as a place of business used by your customers in meetings with you. You must use a portion of your residence regularly and exclusively for either (a) or (b).

Normally you cannot claim a home office if you use the space both for business and personal purposes. One exception: if you use your home as a day-care center, for children, the handicapped, or the elderly. Another exception: You can deduct for the use of a specific area of your home to store goods you sell in your business—even if you occasionally use the storage area for other reasons. The storage space must be the only fixed location of your business—the only place where you could store the goods.

A woman who ran a laundromat could deduct for a home office because she spent most of her time there, did her most important work there, and had a good reason not to set up an office in her laundromat. A musician was allowed to deduct a home office for practicing: His employer didn't provide any practice rooms. A professor could deduct home-office expenses because his office was his main place of business, where he did his research and writing.

The home office must be "separately identifiable," though it needn't be separated from the rest of a room by dividers or curtains. Your office can be in a separate structure, too—a greenhouse, a garage.

Your deductions generally should be based on the space your office occupies compared with the rest of your home—for example, one-tenth. If your rooms are pretty much the same size, you can figure the percentage by dividing the number of rooms used for work by the entire number of rooms in the house.

While tax reform has limited your deductions to your "gross" home-office income, you can carry forward your unused home-office expenses to future years, to offset income from your home business. Your gross income, by the way, isn't quite your gross income. You must first deduct out-of-pocket expenses not linked to your office—what you pay other people, the cost of office supplies.

406 DEDUCT FOR AN OFFICE IF IT HAS OTHER MINOR USES.

For example, you must cross through your office to get to another room. But if the family watches TV in your office, it's no home office.

407 DON'T OVERLOOK ANY DEDUCTIBLE HOME-OFFICE EXPENSES.

Examples: a portion of the cost of repairing the central air-conditioning; the cost of a cleaning person; the entire cost of having your office painted, and a percentage of having the outside painted, the roof or furnace repaired or replaced.

Naturally, you can depreciate the cost of furniture and equipment you use in your office.

Normal expenses you can deduct include the cost of gas, electricity, insurance, depreciation. *Don't* deduct for lawn care. If you deduct for local taxes or mortgage interest, you'll have to subtract those expenses from the overall local taxes and mortgage interest you deduct on Schedule A.

408 STOP DEDUCTING YOUR HOME OFFICE THE YEAR BEFORE YOU SELL.

Otherwise, the profit from the portion of your home you used for an office will not qualify for the deferral tactic or the $125,000 exclusion. Make sure the space you once used as a home office is used for something else now.

409 BE CAREFUL WITH W-2 FORMS.

When an employee retired, his employer filed an inaccurate W-2 form with the IRS, reporting that the man's retirement income was fully taxable—which it wasn't. (He had paid for the retirement income.) He asked his employer to correct the W-2. But his boss never got around to it, and the man was hit with a bill for $15,000 in back taxes, penalties, and interest. Eventually this was straightened out. And the employee successfully sued his boss for his expenses in clearing up the problem and for the value of the time he had spent on the matter.

410 LOWER SOCIAL SECURITY TAXES BY DIVIDING YOUR INCOME.

You must pay Social Security taxes on income up to $48,000 for 1989. Let's say that a couple run the same business. Equal pay may seem fair, but it can cost them in taxes. Let's say that each receives $48,000. Both therefore pay the maximum to Social Security. But if one received $70,000 for doing more work or higher-quality work, and the other $26,000, $22,000 would escape those taxes— $70,000 minus $48,000.

411 TRY TO TURN ITEMIZED DEDUCTIONS INTO BUSINESS EXPENSES.

If you run a small sideline business, your expenses connected with your business are deductible in full, on Schedule C, "Profit or (Loss) From Business or Profession." But many of your itemized deductions, on Schedule A, will be subject to a floor—2 percent of your adjusted gross income. Scrutinize those expenses you've been planning to treat as itemized deductions; maybe they should be treated as deductions related to your business.

412 CONSIDER TURNING BUSINESS INCOME INTO PASSIVE INCOME.

Let's say that you have large passive losses from limited partnerships, and no passive income to write off against those losses. You might hire someone to manage your business, thus converting the business profits into passive income.

413 DON'T DEDUCT 20 PERCENT OF ENTERTAINMENT EXPENSES . . .

if you entertain all your employees at a party in your home. The entire cost is deductible.

414 REMEMBER THAT A BUSINESS DISCUSSION CAN BE EARLY OR LATE . . .

if you're entertaining an out-of-town guest. The usual rule is that, for you to deduct 80 percent of entertainment expenses, a business discussion must be held directly before, during or after. But with an out-of-town visitor, the discussion can take place a day before, or after, the entertainment.

415 REMEMBER THAT THE DISCUSSION RULE DOESN'T APPLY TO MEALS AWAY FROM HOME . . .

when you're away on business, dining alone or with friends, and you deduct only the cost of your meals.

416 CONSIDER TURNING YOUR BUSINESS INTO AN S CORPORATION.

An S corporation must have only thirty-five or fewer shareholders, and must be set up under Subchapter S of the tax code. Such corporations have all sorts of alluring benefits.

The profits of non-S corporations are taxed twice: first to

the corporation, then to the shareholders. With an S corporation, income isn't taxed to the business—just to the shareholders. And S corporation profits are taxed at the shareholders' lower rates (a top of 33 percent in 1989), not at the higher rates (34 percent) that corporations in general currently pay.

If you have losses from a passive investment, you might be able to use an S corporation to throw off passive income, to match against those losses. This would be the case if the S corporation is engaged in any rental activity, or if you don't actively participate in the S corporation.

Another bonus: An S corporation is not subject to the dreaded alternative minimum tax. For non-S corporations, the AMT has jumped to 20 percent from 15 percent. (S corporation shareholders, however, may be subject to the AMT.) Still another bonus: The business can remain on the "cash basis." (Corporations with annual sales of over $5 million must use the "accrual" basis, which means income must be recognized when it's earned, not when you actually get it.) If you're on the cash basis, you can more easily defer income into a future year.

But S corporations have drawbacks, too. They may be taxed on the built-in gains when they convert. They may have to change their tax year—most S corporations must adopt a December 31 year-end—and this may result in a short tax year, with lots of income and few deductions. There can be problems with state taxes. Check with your adviser before going ahead and switching to an S corporation.

417 TAKE AN IMMEDIATE $10,000 WRITE-OFF.

If you buy equipment for your business, you can take the Section 179 ("expensing") deduction—up to $10,000 in the first year. Don't expense business cars. In figuring depreciation, subtract the expensing deduction from the property's basis.

You begin to lose the expensing deduction once you've purchased over $200,000 in new equipment. So try to keep below $200,000 in any year.

418 CARRY OVER ANY EXPENSING YOU HAVEN'T USED.

If your net business income is only $9,000, you can benefit from only $9,000 of expensing. But, you can carry over $1,000 into the next year, to apply against new equipment. Even with the carryover, though, the limit of $10,000 applies. Warnings: You must take the deduction in the year you spend the money—you can't go back and file an amended return. Also, once you make a decision about expensing, describing the property and the part of the purchase price you're writing off, you can't change your mind, decide to expense some other property, and amend your return—unless the IRS gives you permission.

419 USE EXPENSING ON EQUIPMENT YOU MUST DEPRECIATE SLOWLY.

Expense equipment that you must depreciate over seven years, not five years, for example.

420 CHOOSE ACCELERATED DEPRECIATION WHERE YOU CAN.

You can still take accelerated depreciation on certain business items, like computer equipment, put into use after July 31, 1986. (In fact, you can now depreciate them even faster.) And there's a new argument for accelerated depreciation. Time was when you had to pay higher, ordinary-income taxes on profits from the sale of assets that you had depreciated quickly. But because even long-term capital gains are being taxed like ordinary income now, you're not penalized for taking accelerated depreciation. And, of course, the more money you can temporarily save from taxes, the more you'll have to invest.

421 PAY YOUR EMPLOYEES JUST BEFORE THE END OF THE YEAR.

If you're on the cash basis and pay your employees in January for December, you'll have to wait for the following year to deduct the payments. Make out the final weeks' salary checks early, and pay them before the end of the year.

422 TREAT YOUR HOBBY LIKE A BUSINESS.

You can deduct losses from a business—but not from a hobby. In 1986 you could deduct losses from a business only if you had made a profit in *two* of the previous five years. Now you must have made a profit in *three* of the previous five years. (Exception: If you breed horses, you need show a profit in only two of the last seven years for you to qualify as a businessperson, not a hobbyist.)

As a businessperson, you can also deduct expenses on Schedule C, and not have to deduct expenses on Schedule A—expenses that must surpass a 2 percent floor for miscellaneous expenses.

Finally, you can deduct the cost of business trips. If you were a part-time professional photographer last year (you took pictures at weddings, say), write off the cost of visiting trade shows. If you became a part-time professional coin collector, deduct the cost of attending sales and conventions.

To persuade the IRS that your hobby is now a business, set up books and records, and start a separate checking account.

423 GIVE YOUR BUSINESS EXTRA TIME TO PROVE ITSELF.

If your business hasn't made a profit for two years, you can elect to give yourself three more years to make a profit. Use Form 5213.

424 DON'T ASSUME YOUR BUSINESS GENERATES "PASSIVE" INCOME.

Just because your business consists of renting cars or videocassettes, don't assume that it's a passive activity, and you can't write off losses against active income (wages) or portfolio income (capitals gains, interest).

If you "materially" participate in a business, it's not a passive activity. And, by definition, material participation means that you're involved in the "operations" on a "regular, continuous, and substantial" basis. If the business is your main employment, it's a good sign.

Rental businesses that require a lot of work on your part obviously aren't "passive." One clue: There's a lot of turnover (people borrowing and returning videocassettes). Another clue: Your business does more than just rent things. (A car-rental place, for example, must keep the cars running and well maintained—not just rent cars.)

425 SPEND MORE THAN $25 ON A DEDUCTIBLE GIFT.

You're limited to deducting $25 a year for business gifts to individuals. But incidental costs—wrapping a gift, insuring it, mailing it, having it engraved—don't count toward the $25 limit. And if you give someone a $25 present, you can also give him or her an item costing less than $4 that has your business name on it (like pencils and pens) without surpassing the $25.

426 THINK TWICE BEFORE PAYING A PREMIUM FOR CHOICE TICKETS.

The show is sold out? You'll have to pay a huge markup for tickets? Hesitate. You can deduct only 80 percent of the tickets' face value—and none of the premium.

427 DEDUCT FOR ATTENDING BUSINESS CONVENTIONS.

Don't confuse investment seminars with business meetings. You can no longer deduct the cost of traveling to investment seminars, or a seminar's registration fees. But you can still deduct the travel costs, lodgings, registration fees, 80 percent of meals, and so forth when you attend seminars, meetings, or conventions related to your business.

428 DON'T INCLUDE AS INCOME ORDERS YOU HAVEN'T FILLED.

Even if you're on the accrual basis, you don't have to declare income until a sale is completed. So, even if you have orders on hand and merchandise ready for shipment, you needn't report any income until the merchandise is on the way.

429 DON'T INCLUDE PAYMENTS-IN-ADVANCE IN THIS YEAR'S INCOME.

If you're on the accrual basis, and you receive an advance payment in 1989 for work you'll do in 1990, it's income in 1990. (But if you're on the cash basis, it's 1989 income.)

430 DON'T OVERVALUE YOUR INVENTORY.

The cost of your goods isn't just the invoice price, minus any trade discounts. Also add freight charges or other expenses in getting the merchandise to your place of business.

431 DON'T INCLUDE MERCHANDISE YOU HAVEN'T PAID FOR.

Don't include in your inventory any goods you received in December if you didn't receive the bills until January. If you do, you're needlessly increasing your previous year's income by the cost of the goods. Even if you receive the bills in January, treat them as purchases you made in December. That expense will offset the value of the goods.

432 DEDUCT EVEN PARTIAL BUSINESS BAD DEBTS.

Don't confuse a business bad debt with a personal bad debt, which must be *totally* worthless to be deductible.

433 DEDUCT FOR BAD DEBTS AS SOON AS POSSIBLE.

You can take a loss for a bad debt only in the year when the obligation becomes worthless—not in a later year. (But

you can amend your return for the earlier year.) So don't
put it off. Signs that a debt is worthless: the debtor declared
bankruptcy; he or she went out of business; a judgment
against the debtor can't be collected.

434 DEDUCT CASUALTY LOSSES IN FULL.

In deducting business property that's stolen or destroyed,
you need not subtract $100, then 10 percent of your adjusted
gross income, as you must with personal property. Deduct
the full amount of the loss, on Schedule C.

435 DEDUCT YOUR SECURITY DEPOSIT . . .

on business premises that you rent, as an advance rental
payment—provided that this is in accord with your lease.
This way, you get a deduction and your landlord may get
more passive income to offset against any losses.

436 DEDUCT THE COST OF A WATCHDOG.

Include the cost of food and veterinary bills. (Expenses for
a seeing-eye dog are medical deductions.)

437 DON'T OVERLOOK ANY OTHER BUSINESS EXPENSES.

Some that you might forget: donations to business organizations; payments to nonemployees for research, typing,
consulting, and so forth; license fees; postage; education
expenses; and certain lobbying expenses.

Chapter Fourteen
PARENTS AND THE DIVORCED

The "kiddie" tax has proved to be quite a burden. Some parents who put money into their children's names, for their college educations, are now having to make estimated-tax payments for their little kids.

The "kiddie" tax refers to the fact that you can no longer give stocks, bonds, and money to children under fourteen and have all that wealth grow in value while being fully taxed at the kids' low rates.

Tax reform mandated that a child's unearned income—interest, dividends, rents, royalties, and so forth—will be taxed (beyond $1,000) at the tax rate of the parent. If the parents are divorced or separated, it's the rate of the custodial parent that counts. And if the custodial parent is married and files a joint return, you must use the joint taxable income in calculating the child's tax on investment income.

Why the special $1,000? The standard deduction provides $500, and the next $500 is taxed at the child's own tax rate—typically 15 percent for 1989. A child's earned income (from a job), though, will always be taxed at the child's rate.

Clifford trusts and other income-shifting devices are also out the window. And, the final blow, if you can take a child as an exemption, the child cannot claim an exemption for himself or herself.

No, this doesn't mean that you shouldn't begin saving for a child's college education, or just for the child's future well-being, until the kid is fourteen. The rules are stricter, and your options more limited, but you can still do a lot for your child—before and after the child is fourteen.

Important: If your child's income is taxed at your rate, it doesn't affect your credits or deductions. It doesn't raise your adjusted gross income for the various floors (such as the 2 percent floor on miscellaneous deductions), and it doesn't affect the phaseout on a parent's right to the $25,000 allowance for passive losses.

438 ADD YOUR CHILD'S INVESTMENT INCOME TO YOUR OWN.

Save yourself the trouble of doing your kid's return. You can now add a dependent's investment income over $1,000 to your own return if the dependent was under fourteen on January 1. The child's gross income for 1989 had to be over $500 and less than $5,000. Also, the child cannot have made estimated tax payments, and no Federal tax could have been withheld from his income. Also, none of the child's overpayment for 1988 could have been applied to 1989. File Form 8814.

439 REMEMBER THAT $1,000 A YEAR CAN AMOUNT TO A LOT.

You can give a child a $12,500 certificate of deposit yielding 8 percent—and, the first year, it would provide the child with about $1,000 in income, all taxed at the child's rate.

These days, the average stock yields 3 percent in dividends. That means a child could have $33,333 in stocks, yielding $1,000.

Of course, these yields would quickly rise over $1,000 after the first year. But the point is that $1,000 in unearned income implies a principal that's not to be sneezed at. So you should consider starting a college education fund way before a child reaches fourteen.

Keep in mind, too, that $1,000 a year, with half untaxed and half taxed at 15 percent, can grow into a decent piece of change. It would be significantly more than your investing $1,000 a year in your own name, taxed at 15 percent, 28 percent, or 33 percent (the rates in 1988 and after).

440 REMEMBER: A CHILD CAN TAKE MORE THAN THE $500 STANDARD DEDUCTION.

If the child's itemized deductions, relating to unearned income, exceed $500, the child can take the higher figure instead. Such deductions might include custodial fees and investment guidance. Also, if a child's earned income is over $500, the standard deduction equals the earned income—up to $3,100 for 1989.

441 CONSIDER GIVING $10,000 A YEAR TO A CHILD.

Why $10,000? Because that's the amount not subject to gift taxes that the giver might otherwise have to pay. If you and your spouse combine on a gift, it can be $20,000 a year, untaxed. And that's $20,000 a year *to each child*.

You might want to wait until a child is fourteen before beginning to give large amounts—when the earnings will be taxed at the child's rate. And giving $20,000 a year to a child of fourteen means that just the principal will be $80,000 when the child is eighteen and about to jaunt off to college. At 10 percent interest, the child would have around $102,000. That should help defray a few expenses.

There's another reason, of course, to give away assets to a child: so the assets won't be taxed as part of your estate when you die.

442   QUICKLY GIVE A CHILD $40,000, TAX-FREE.

You and your spouse can give a child a total of $20,000 at the end of one year, and another $20,000 at the beginning of the next.

443   LEND A CHILD $10,000, INTEREST-FREE.

Let's say that your son or daughter is entering college. You can make your child an interest-free loan of up to $10,000, which he or she can quickly pay to the college. Later on, your child will repay the loan.

Usually, if you make an interest-free loan, for tax purposes you're considered to have received the going rate of interest, and the person who received the loan is considered to have paid the going rate of interest. But not in this case. A loan of $10,000 to your child is tax-free as long as one of the principal reasons for the loan is not tax-avoidance—and none of the money will be used for income-producing investments.

444 SET UP A CUSTODIAL ACCOUNT.

It's a snap. Just visit or write to a bank, brokerage firm, or mutual fund. You can put cash, stocks, bonds, or other income-producing assets into a custodial account.

Ideally, the custodian won't be a parent but a trusted friend or relative. Otherwise, if the parent who made the gift and who serves as custodian dies before the child reaches legal adulthood, the account may be included in the parent's gross estate for estate-tax purposes.

The child will assume control of the account when he or she reaches eighteen or twenty-one, depending on state law.

If you use the account to cover expenses you're legally obligated to pay for—a child's food, medical expenses, shelter, and clothing, for instance—the account's income to that extent will be taxed to the parent. In some states, a wealthy parent is required to pay for a child's education—which means that you, as custodian, couldn't use the money for college expenses without owing taxes. But if children reach legal adulthood at eighteen, just when they are entering college, they themselves can use the money to pay for their college expenses. And in most states, eighteen is the legal age of adulthood.

445 CONSIDER GROWTH STOCKS.

One advantage of giving a child stocks is that no taxes need be paid on the stocks' appreciation until you sell them. So, if you put stocks into a child's name, the appreciation can build up—untaxed—year after year.

True, stocks do pay taxable dividends. But small-company or growth stocks pay little if any, and over the years, growth stocks have fared better than blue chips (stocks of older, bigger companies). You might be best off buying a child shares of a mutual fund that specializes in growth stocks. The fund will sell some of them over the years, triggering taxable gains. But perhaps the fund's improved performance—thanks to its buying and selling—will offset the taxes your child will have to pay on the distributions.

Warning: The stock market can, and has, gone down and stayed there. In 1973–1974, stocks lost almost 50 percent of their value. But stock-market declines rarely have lasted for more than four years. So, if you buy stocks for a very young child, intending to cover his or her college education, you can start selling them when the child is fourteen, fifteen, sixteen, seventeen, or eighteen. During at least one of those years, the market should be high. And once children are nearing college age, and their unearned income is taxed at their own rates, you might put their holdings into very safe, stable investments—like short-term bonds, money-market funds, or certificates of deposit.

446 GIVE A CHILD APPRECIATED PROPERTY.

Up to $18,550 of the income of a child fourteen or older is taxed at a 15 percent rate for 1989. And if you give your child stocks or other assets on which you have capital gains, the child can sell them and pay taxes on the gain at the child's lower tax rate.

447 GIVE A CHILD STOCK IN YOUR COMPANY.

If your family owns a company, give your children stock—$10,000/$20,000 a year, so you won't be subject to gift taxes. If the stock pays no dividends, the child will owe no taxes. When the child reaches fourteen, rebuy the stock. (Or spread out your repurchases over a few years if the child might otherwise wind up in the 28 or 33 percent bracket because of high capital gains.)

448 CONSIDER ZERO-COUPON CORPORATE BONDS.

Interest on these bonds (see Chapter 8) accumulates slowly. Annual interest will be less than $1,000 for the first thirteen years on $30,000 face value 8 percent bonds due in eighteen years. You could thus buy taxable zeros for a young child and keep the taxes low for the life of the bond.

449 CONSIDER TAX-DEFERRED OR TAX-EXEMPT INVESTMENTS.

A suitable tax-deferred investment you might put into a child's name: Series EE bonds (see Chapter 8).

If you're not far from fifty-nine and a half, or if the grandparents are interested, you or they might purchase an annuity, withdrawing the investment to pay for a child's education. You usually must pay a 10 percent penalty on the withdrawal if you take out money from the annuity before you're fifty-nine and a half.

Other suitable tax-exempt investments include municipal bonds, municipal bond mutual funds, municipal bond unit trusts, and zero-coupon municipal bonds.

450 CONSIDER AN IRREVOCABLE TRUST.

People setting up new trusts will have the income taxed at their own tax rates if the trust money ever reverts to them, or if they can control the trust in any way. But you can still have trust money taxed to the trust if you give up all your rights to your gift—the gift is irrevocable.

Trusts are taxed at a rate of 15 percent on the first $5,000 of income, and above that at 28 percent. (The benefit of the 15 percent rate is phased out by a surcharge as income grows from $13,000 to $26,000.) Those rates may be lower than yours.

Another possible benefit of a trust: You can put real estate into it—which you cannot always do with a custodial account.

With a 2503(c) trust, the money is turned over to the child when he or she reaches eighteen or twenty-one, depending on the law in your state. A lawyer may charge a few hundred dollars to set up such a trust.

An interesting variation on an irrevocable trust: Set up a trust for your needy parents for ten years or so. At the end of that time, the trust could revert to your child. The only people subject to taxes on the income will be your parents— who are probably in a low tax bracket anyway.

451 GIVE YOUR CHILD A JOB.

If you're self-employed, or you have a part-time freelance job, hire your child, particularly if he or she is under fourteen. You'll keep money in the family that way.

Pay the child up to $5,100 (for 1989), and you won't owe any taxes (apart from Social Security if the child is over seventeen). Reason: A child who works has a $3,100 standard deduction, and can salt away $2,000 into a deductible IRA.

Pay the child a reasonable wage—not ridiculously high— and you can deduct it from your own income.

You need not pay Social Security taxes for a child under eighteen, if your business isn't incorporated.

Just don't try getting away with deducting the cost of paying a child to do his or her homework.

Even if your child works for you, you can claim the child as dependent if he or she is under nineteen or a full-time student, and you provide more than half the total support.

452 FUND A CHILD'S IRA.

If a person puts away $2,000 into an IRA from age nineteen to twenty-six, and *stops,* he or she will have $1,035,160 at age sixty-five (assuming the money compounded at 10 percent a year). If the person starts at age twenty-seven, and *continues* putting $2,000 into an IRA every year until he or she is sixty-five, he or she will have less—$883,185. In short, the younger you begin an IRA investment program, the better.

453 HAVE THE LOWER-EARNING DIVORCÉ(E) CLAIM THE CHILD DEPENDENCY.

Consider having the lower-earning parent claim the child as a dependent. Reason: Beginning in 1988, high-earners (in the 33 percent bracket) gradually lose personal exemptions for themselves and their children as their income climbs. But the lower-earning parent may still benefit. In the past, the higher-earning parent usually wanted the exemption, because he or she was in a higher tax bracket.

454 CONSIDER A NEW ALIMONY ARRANGEMENT.

Before tax reform, you could deduct $10,000 for alimony you paid; anything beyond $10,000 was deductible only if you were required to make payments for six or more years.

Now you can deduct as much as $15,000 a year; amounts over that are deductible if they're made for at least three years, and are regular enough not to look like lump-sum payments.

What this means is that you can arrange to make more generous payments over a shorter period of time, boosting your early deductions. And remember that alimony you pay lowers your adjusted gross income—which helps you itemize, and helps you surpass the floors for medical expenses, casualty losses, and certain miscellaneous expenses.

455 BE WARY OF RECEIVING PROPERTY IN A DIVORCE.

If you receive property—say, a house—you won't have to pay income taxes when you receive it. But when you sell, you'll pay—and your basis (total investment) will be the price of the house when your spouse purchased it, not the date you received it. And remember that capital-gains taxes are equal to the rates on ordinary income. Cash might be better, because you would pay less taxes on account of the decline in tax rates. So, if your ex wants to give you property, ask for extra concessions.

If you're making the alimony payments, though, you may prefer to give property. Reason: Alimony payments are worth less now that tax rates have gone down.

So you and your ex may have some serious talking to do. Many existing divorce decrees and separation agreements can be renegotiated when there's a big change in the tax law.

456 MAKE SURE THAT YOUR ALIMONY PAYMENTS ARE DEDUCTIBLE.

The rules governing divorce decrees and separate-maintenance agreements before 1985 differ from those later on. For payments under a decree of divorce or agreement *after* 1984 to be deductible, payments must be in cash, not in property.

457 CONSIDER FUNDING AN IRA WITH ALIMONY YOU RECEIVE.

You're allowed to fund an individual retirement arrangement with the alimony you receive, as if it were earned income.

458 DON'T GIVE YOUR EX-SPOUSE AN ANNUITY.

It won't qualify as alimony because it's considered property, and you cannot deduct property as alimony. But the paying spouse could obtain an annuity, give the payments he or she receives to the ex-spouse, then deduct the payments as alimony.

459 REMEMBER THAT YOU CAN BE FLEXIBLE.

Normally, alimony you pay is deductible; alimony you receive is taxable. But what if the paying spouse wants to be generous—and not deduct the alimony and not have the ex-spouse pay taxes on it as income?

That can be arranged. The divorce decree or separation agreement can specify that a payment won't qualify as alimony for tax purposes, and the IRS will go along.

460 DEDUCT LEGAL COSTS . . .

of a divorce insofar as they were for obtaining alimony payments or for tax advice. They are miscellaneous expenses, subject to the floor of 2 percent of your adjusted gross income. You can also deduct the cost of getting your ex-spouse to make the payments he or she owes.

461 DEDUCT THE ENTIRE AMOUNT OF ALIMONY . . .

even if part of it goes for child support, so long as your legal arrangement didn't specify that a certain portion go to any children.

Chapter Fifteen
RETIREMENT

Thanks to tax reform, the argument for retirement planning has become even more compelling. One reason is that, apart from retirement plans, there are hardly any other tax shelters left. Another reason: Contributions to deductible retirement plans can lower your adjusted gross income—and thus enable you to itemize, and enable your deductions to surpass the floors for medical expenses, casualty losses, and miscellaneous deductions.

Tax reform has helped the retirement-minded in other ways, too. Now you can withdraw money from an IRA before age fifty-nine and a half, without penalty, if you "annuitize" the payments—receive them in line with your projected lifespan. And if your spouse earns less than $250, you can put an extra $250 into a spousal IRA.

On the other hand, tax reform has seen to it that, for about 10 percent of the population, contributions to individual retirement arrangements are no longer deductible. The new law has also lowered the maximum you can contribute to a salary-reduction plan, and cut back on the special income-averaging of lump-sum pension distributions.

Even so, our best piece of advice for you is to

462 FUND A RETIREMENT PLAN.

The key benefit of putting money into a retirement plan is that your contributions will grow, tax-deferred. And while you may be in the 28 or 33 percent tax bracket in 1989, you might be in the 15 percent bracket years from now, when you withdraw your money—and thus save a bundle on the total taxes you will pay.

You can also fund your pension plan with pre-tax dollars, as with a deductible IRA or a salary-reduction plan, like a 401(k) plan or a Section 403(b) plan (for those who work for qualified nonprofit organizations).

People keep wondering how to invest their retirement money. My general advice is: If you're young, consider stocks. Stocks, in the long run, have performed far better than bonds and money-market instruments. But note that I said "in the long run." If you're young, you can wait out the usual stomach-turning stock-market declines. I recommend that young people invest in no-load stock mutual funds with good long-term records.

But if you're getting on in years, you should probably tilt toward fixed-interest investments, like bonds or certificates of deposit. You don't want to find yourself needing your retirement money to live on just when the stock market is in the doldrums. Vary your bonds' maturities: Have some short-term, some intermediate-term, some long-term. Short-term usually means a year to five years; intermediate-term, five to ten years; and long-term is anything over that. The conservative might want to skip long-term bonds altogether.

The return they give may not be enough to offset the risk of their value's plummeting if interest rates climb.

If you need every cent from your pension, and can't afford any risk whatever, consider money-market funds. Inflation can shrink the money you have even in short-term bonds.

Still, a good case can be made for diversifying. Young people might purchase fixed-return investments, especially if they're not familiar with the ups and downs of the stock market, and might panic in a downturn. Older people not in straitened circumstances might own some good stocks or stock mutual funds, along with their fixed-income investments. Stocks and stock mutual funds offer some protection against inflation; they offer the greatest possibility of appreciation; and they're fun to follow. Just remember: The worst mistake you can make when you buy stocks is to panic when the market goes down, and sell your holdings.

463 FUND A 401(K) PLAN.

Salary-reduction or 401(k) plans are absolutely wonderful—better even than deductible IRAs. You can put more money away—up to $7,627 (as of 1989; the amount will rise with the Consumer Price Index) or 20 percent of your income, whichever is less. (You can salt away even *more* into a 403[b] plan.) Your contribution is automatically deducted from your salary. And although it's subject to Social Security taxes, it's immune to current income taxes. (This isn't true of some other employer-sponsored thrift plans, in which your contributions are made with post-tax money.) You can even borrow some of your investment, which you can't do with an IRA.

As if all these benefits weren't enough, many employers kick in a contribution of their own, typically as high as 50 percent of your contribution, though perhaps up to a cutoff point.

Beg or borrow (draw the line at stealing), but do fund your 401(k) plan. If your employer kicks in 20 percent, or 50 percent, a 401(k) is too tempting to pass up.

Your $7,627 limit (as of 1989) doesn't include your employer's contribution. But your employer's contribution *does* count toward the limit of 20 percent of your salary. (Most people I know put away 5 to 15 percent.) In fact, if you also have access to a Simplified Employee Pension where you work, your contributions to the SEP count toward your current total $7,627 limit, as do contributions you make to other employer-sponsored retirement arrangements.

Borrowing from your 401(k) plan should be done only with the best of reasons—like buying a house. The rules are a bit complicated.

Tax reform requires you to pay back your loan within five years, unless you're borrowing to buy a home for yourself (not for a child or other relative). You must repay the loan in level quarterly installments. If you borrow $5,000, you must repay at least $1,000 a year, $250 every four months, plus interest.

The old rule was that you could borrow half your pension assets, up to $50,000; but you could always borrow $10,000. Now the amount you can borrow depends on what you've borrowed in the previous twelve months.

Let's say you have $100,000 in your plan (lucky you), and you theoretically could borrow half, or $50,000. You've borrowed $40,000, then repaid it. But within the next year, you borrow another $10,000. Now you want to borrow more.

Take the $50,000 limit and subtract: $40,000 minus $10,000, or $30,000. You can borrow $20,000. Before tax reform, you could have borrowed $40,000 (the $50,000 limit minus the existing $10,000 loan).

Obviously, the IRS wants to discourage frequent borrowings from pension plans.

The rules on withdrawing money from 401(k)s before age fifty-nine and a half are strict. You can permanently take out your assets for "financial hardship," if you leave the company, or if you're disabled.

If you withdraw money from a 401(k) for financial hardship, or because you left the company, you'll have to pay a 10 percent penalty on the amount you withdraw, along with regular income taxes. Exception: If your withdrawal is to pay for medical expenses that qualify as tax deductible, there's no penalty. (But starting in 1989, even in these circumstances you cannot withdraw your earnings on your contributions.)

You can use special lump-sum averaging on withdrawals if (a) you're fifty-nine and a half, or you were at least 50 on January 1, 1986, (b) you take a lump-sum distribution, and (c) you belonged to the plan for at least five years.

464 FUND A DEDUCTIBLE IRA.

Even if your salary is in the millions, you can deduct your IRA contribution *so long as neither you nor your spouse was an active member of a qualified employer-sponsored pension plan.* Such plans include 401(k) plans; pension, profit-sharing, and stock-bonus plans; Keoghs or HR-10s; annuity plans; Simplified Employee Benefit Plans; and 501(c)(18) union pension plans.

If you, or your spouse, participate in a company retirement plan, you can still deduct a full $2,000 IRA contribution if your adjusted gross income was $40,000 or less. If you're single or a head of household, the cutoff is $25,000. If you're married, you can deduct *some* of your IRA contribution if your adjusted gross income is less than $50,000;

the same is true of a single person whose adjusted gross income is below $35,000. In calculating your adjusted gross income, do *not* subtract your IRA contributions.

For every $1 your adjusted gross income exceeds $40,000/$25,000, you lose 20 cents of your deduction. Let's say your adjusted gross income is $46,000 and you're filing jointly. You're $6,000 above the limit. Multiply the $6,000 by 20 cents, to get $1,200. Subtract that from $2,000—and you wind up with the amount you can deduct, $800. (But you can still put $1,200—$2,000 minus $800—into a *nondeductible* IRA.) Suppose your adjusted gross income is $49,000. Multiply $9,000 by 20 cents, and you get $1,800. You can deduct only $200.

The most you can salt away into an IRA during one year, for yourself, is $2,000, or 100 percent of your earned income, whichever is less. Dividends, interest, capital gains, and such don't qualify as earned income, though alimony does.

Okay, a key question is: Are you or aren't you a participant in a qualified retirement plan? If you elect to join a 401(k) plan and part of your salary is deferred, you're a participant. In fact, you don't have to participate actively to be considered a participant in a plan; if you're eligible, you're ineligible for a deductible IRA. So is your spouse, even if he/she isn't covered.

If you belong to a profit-sharing plan, though, and there were no profits that went your way, you're not a participant. The same is true if you're in a stock-bonus plan, and received no stock.

Check with your employer if you're not sure whether or not you actively participate in a plan. And you *may* not be sure if you left your place of employment during the year.

You cannot invest your IRA in collectibles, antiques, art, stamps, or precious metals. An exception: gold or silver coins issued by the government.

465 WITHDRAW YOUR IRA MONEY WHEN YOU MUST.

By April 1 of the year after you reach seventy and a half, you must start withdrawing money from your IRAs. Otherwise, you face a stiff penalty—50 percent of the difference between what you should have withdrawn and what you did take out. If you take out money in installments, it must all have been withdrawn by the end of your estimated lifespan. But don't worry that you'll outlive your money. The amount you must withdraw changes as you age. After all, the longer you live, the longer your estimated lifespan. (Your IRA's custodian will have tables showing estimated lifespans.)

466 NAME A YOUNGER BENEFICIARY.

If you want to lower your withdrawal rate, because you want the money to continue compounding tax-free, name a younger beneficiary. If you're married, you can use the longer lifespans based on your life expectancy together with your spouse's, assuming that your spouse is the beneficiary.

You can also name a person younger than your spouse as beneficiary. But you must withdraw at least 50 percent of the account during your lifetime, no matter what your beneficiary's age.

You must now use a ten-year rule: For the payout schedule, you must consider the age of your beneficiary to be no more than ten years below yours. Exception: If the beneficiary is your spouse, you can use his or her real age, no matter how young.

Warning: If you change beneficiaries, the age of the first beneficiary is binding as far as the payout schedule goes.

You cannot contribute to an IRA past the time you reach seventy and a half. But if your spouse is under seventy and

a half and unemployed, you can continue contributing to a
spousal IRA on his or her behalf if you have earned income.

467 COORDINATE WITHDRAWALS WITH SOCIAL SECURITY PAYMENTS.

If a married couple's income, minus certain adjustments,
surpasses $32,000, part of their Social Security payments
becomes taxable. The figure for a single person: $25,000.
So, try to keep your pension-plan withdrawals low enough
so as not to trigger a tax on any of your Social Security
income.

468 TRY FOR A PARTIAL DEDUCTION.

Avoid the mistake of thinking you must contribute the whole
$2,000 to an IRA to get, say, an $800 partial deduction. For
an $800 partial deduction you're entitled to (a single person
with an AGI of $31,000), you need contribute only $800.
(Multiply $6,000 by 0.2, subtract the $1,200 from $2,000.)

469 DON'T PUT SHORT-TERM MONEY INTO AN IRA.

Put money into an IRA only if you're pretty sure you won't
be needing it till you're at least fifty-nine and a half. If you
withdraw your IRA funds prematurely (you're not fifty-nine
and a half or disabled, or you don't take the payments in
amounts geared to your estimated lifespan), you face a 10
percent tax penalty on the amount you withdraw, along with
regular income taxes. (You won't pay taxes on your
principal if you withdraw funds from a nondeductible IRA.
But if you have both deductible and nondeductible IRAs,

any withdrawal is considered to come partially from both.)
You would have to keep an IRA for many years—about
thirteen—before your earnings would overcome that 10
percent penalty.

470 DON'T PUT TAX-EXEMPT INVESTMENTS INTO AN IRA.

Yes, some people put tax-free municipal bonds into IRAs.
This is redundant, because IRA contributions grow tax-
deferred anyway. It's also disastrous: Whatever you
withdraw from an IRA is taxed as if it were ordinary
income. So your tax-free municipal-bond interest would be
taxed as soon as it left your IRA!

471 BORROW TO FUND YOUR IRA.

All of the interest on a loan to fund an IRA may be deductible as investment interest, the IRS has ruled. That gives you
an incentive to borrow to fund your IRA, if you don't have
the money available—particularly if your IRA contribution
itself is still deductible.

But with the lowering of tax brackets, this step may not
make as much financial sense as before. You don't save as
much taxes as you used to, when tax brackets were higher.
You must consider the interest, dividends, and possible
appreciation of your IRA.

So, rather than borrowing from a bank, find a really cheap
source of money, like a loan from any whole-life insurance
policy you have. An even cheaper source: borrowing from
yourself. Roll over an existing IRA; use the money to fund
your new IRA; then, when you have more money, put the
amount you withdrew into the rollover IRA. Do it within

sixty days of your borrowing the money, so you won't have
a tax liability and a penalty.

472 TAKE THE $200 IRA DEDUCTION.

Let's say that you're married, filing a joint return, and your
adjusted gross income is $49,500. Poor you, according to
the calculations, you can deduct only $100. The IRS,
though, lets you deduct $200—just as long as your adjusted
gross income is below $50,000. Remember this break if your
adjusted gross income is over $49,000 for 1989. And if
you're single or the head of a household, remember the $200
deduction if your adjusted gross income is over $34,000.

473 FUND A SPOUSAL IRA.

You work, earning at least $2,250 a year, but your spouse
doesn't work at all. Or you work, but your spouse earns less
than $250 a year. The upshot is that you can salt away
$2,250 into deductible IRAs. You can put $2,000 in your
name, or in your spouse's name; you can put the balance of
the $2,250 in the other person's name. But you cannot put
more than $2,000 into one account. If it's a nondeductible
IRA, you might put most of it into the IRA of the spouse
with not many deductible IRAs. That way, you can
withdraw some money before you're fifty-nine and a half,
and pay less tax and penalty—because you've withdrawn
proportionately less from deductible IRAs.

And think about hiring your spouse, so he or she can fund
an IRA—which may be deductible if you're not a member
of a qualified employer-sponsored retirement plan or if your
income is below the threshold. Some sole proprietors hire

their spouses to help out in the office, paying them at least
$2,000 a year.

474 DEDUCT CUSTODIAL FEES.

You can deduct fees you pay a custodian during the year to
manage your IRA if they are "ordinary and necessary."
They're "miscellaneous" deductions, subject to a reduction
of 2 percent of your adjusted gross income.

475 TRANSFER YOUR IRAS FOR HIGHER RETURNS.

At IRA time (January to April 15), some banks offer certificates of deposit paying high interest. Then, once they have
lured in lots of IRA money, they let their interest rates sink,
compared to what other banks are paying, trusting that
depositors will remain with them, out of inertia. But you can
transfer your account from custodian to custodian as often
as you like, as long as you yourself don't have access to the
money. So ask a bank paying a competitive interest rate to
handle the transfer. That will spare you some paperwork—
and enable you to transfer your IRA later the same year, if
you like. And remember: You aren't limited to banks in
your area. In fact, you aren't limited to banks. Consider
stockbrokers and mutual funds.

You can make as many trustee-to-trustee IRA transfers as
you like; but you're limited to one rollover per account a
year. (In a rollover, you get direct access to the funds.)

476 CONSIDER A NONDEDUCTIBLE IRA.

Why not a municipal-bond fund instead? A muni fund would
be liquid—you could get the money if you needed it, without

tax penalties. And when you retrieve all your interest, you wouldn't pay a penny in taxes—whereas the interest and appreciation on an IRA investment would be taxed as regular income.

There are two arguments in favor of nondeductible IRAs: (1) You can earn more on your money. Corporate bonds, for example, pay more than munis—and they can be just as safe or safer, if you stick with high-rated issues. In fact, if you put a nondeductible IRA in a growth or aggressive-growth mutual fund with a good record, like Twentieth Century Select or Fidelity Magellan, you may make out like a bandit—and all of your gains will be tax-deferred. (2) You may not want such easy access to your money.

Of course, there's nothing wrong with having a liquid municipal-bond fund—along with a nondeductible IRA in a higher-paying investment.

477 FORWARD-AVERAGE A LUMP-SUM DISTRIBUTION.

If you leave your employer, receive all of your pension-plan assets in one lump sum, and meet certain other conditions, there's a way to avoid being taxed on the entire amount at your highest tax rate.

Before tax reform, you would calculate the tax on one-tenth the amount, multiply it by ten, and that was your one-time tax on the distribution. Confused? Remember, there were lots of tax brackets way back when. One-tenth of the distribution very likely fell into a low tax bracket. Multiplying that tax by ten was probably far less than the tax on the entire amount, at the higher tax bracket.

Tax reform, though, abolished that special break—unless you were fifty years old or older on January 1, 1986. In that case, you can choose between ten-year averaging and five-year averaging of a lump-sum distribution. (If you're below fifty-nine and a half, you can never use this break again.)

The choice between ten-year averaging and five-year averaging isn't simple. Ten-year averaging is based on the higher tax rates of 1986; five-year averaging is based on the new, lower tax rates. You'll have to figure it out both ways to see which is better for you.

Those who weren't at least fifty on that date can choose only five-year income-averaging once they're fifty-nine and a half or older. Your tax on a lump-sum distribution is five times what the tax is on one-fifth the distribution. Let's hope that, in 1989, one-fifth of any distribution you receive falls within the 15 percent bracket, and not the 28 percent or the 33 percent brackets. You can use five-year averaging only once, and only after you've reached fifty-nine and a half.

478 AVOID THE 10 PERCENT PENALTY ON LUMP-SUM DISTRIBUTIONS.

You'll face that penalty if you withdraw your pension money before you're fifty-nine and a half, even if the reason is that you've left your job. (But there's no penalty if you withdrew the money because you were disabled.)

One solution: You can roll over the money into an IRA (see below). Or, if you get a new job, you can roll over the lump sum into your new employer's pension plan, if you have your new employer's permission. Or, if you've left your job, you can choose to have the lump sum taken as an annuity. Finally, if you're at least fifty-five and take early retirement under your company's plan, the penalty doesn't apply.

479 HAVE YOUR DISTRIBUTION TAXED AS CAPITAL GAINS.

Before tax reform, if you had contributions to your pension plan before 1974, you could treat part of your distribution as a long-term gain, which is taxed leniently. You figured out the ratio of your pre-1974 investment years and your post-1974 investment years.

Now this favorable treatment of pre-1974 gains is being phased out. If you take out your pension money in 1989, 75 percent is taxed favorably. In 1990, it's 50 percent. In 1991, it's 25 percent. In 1992, the special break vanishes entirely. But if you were fifty or more on January 1, 1986, all of pre-1974 contributions will still be taxed leniently—whatever the year you receive your distributions. The tax rate will be a straight 20 percent; it doesn't vary according to your tax bracket.

480 ROLL OVER A DISTRIBUTION.

You leave your job, or your company goes out of business. Right now, you don't need the $50,000 (or whatever) the company gives you, and you don't expect to need it over the next few years. You don't want to pay taxes on it, and you do want it to continue appreciating. Your best course is to roll over the distribution into an IRA. (Lump sums aren't subject to the usual $2,000 limit.) There's no tax bite if you do it within sixty days of your getting the distribution. Inform your new custodian—bank, savings and loan, stockbroker, mutual fund—that this is a rollover IRA.

Warning: By rolling-over a lump-sum distribution, you lose the right ever to use special forward-averaging on the distribution. Money withdrawn from an IRA cannot be forward-averaged. But if you won't need the money for years, a rollover will still usually give you more money in the long run.

481 CONSIDER A KEOGH.

The self-employed should consider Keogh plans, or HR-10 plans, as the IRS prefers them to be known.

You can deduct your contribution from your income. And your contributions grow, tax-deferred.

You must set up a Keogh before the end of the year, though; you cannot contribute to one in 1990 unless you made the arrangements in 1989—although you can do that with a Simplified Employee Pension plan or an IRA.

Among the types of Keoghs:

DEFINED CONTRIBUTION. With a *profit-sharing plan*, you can put in whichever is lower: up to $30,000 every year, or up to 15 percent of your earnings (minus pension-plan contributions). Here's how to figure out your Keogh contribution: Multiply your net earned income by 15 percent; divide the result by 1.15. That's your maximum, providing it's not over $30,000. Example: You netted $50,000. Multiply that by 15 percent, which gives you $7,500. Dividing by 1.15 gives you $6,521—your deductible contribution. Or just multiply the net earned income by 13.043 percent.

With a profit-sharing plan, you can vary the amounts you put into your Keogh.

With a *money-purchase plan,* you can contribute 25 percent of your net earnings. Here, you divide by 1.25. If you net $50,000, you can contribute $10,000 ($50,000 times 25 percent divided by 1.25). Or just multiply your net earned income by 20 percent.

With a money-purchase plan, you must contribute a fixed percentage of your income every year.

DEFINED BENEFIT. This is a lot more complicated than a defined-contribution plan. What you contribute depends upon what you'd like to withdraw every year when you retire, and that amount will depend upon your life expectancy and your age. The annual benefit when you retire can't exceed more than $94,023—or your average earnings for the three consecutive working years during which you earned the most money whichever is less.

Tax reform has lowered the income you can receive from a defined-benefit plan if you retire earlier than sixty-five.

The trouble with defined-benefit plans is that they lock you into making a set contribution—whether you can afford it or not. They're best for people getting on in years, who can afford several years of high payments.

You must start withdrawing your Keogh money by age seventy and a half, either in installments or all at once. If you withdraw your money in a lump sum, you can take advantage of the special forward-averaging formula.

You can fund a Keogh—or a SEP (see below)—even if you're salaried, so long as you also have some self-employment income.

482 ROLL OVER DISTRIBUTIONS INTO A KEOGH.

There's a good reason to roll over a distribution into a Keogh instead of an IRA. You can use special lump-sum averaging on the proceeds from a Keogh, but not on proceeds from an IRA.

483 DEFER FUNDING YOUR KEOGH.

You don't have enough money to fund a Keogh? If you file early, you can nonetheless deduct for a Keogh contribution—and, if you have tax money coming to you, use the refund to finally fund your plan. (The IRS trusts you to do as you promised.)

Or you can file for a four-month automatic extension of the due date of your return, meanwhile paying all of your tax bill. Then you'll have an extra four months to fund your Keogh. This extension tactic doesn't work with IRAs.

484 CONSIDER A SEP.

If you're self-employed, you can set up a SEP, which doesn't have the onerous reporting requirements of a Keogh. Another advantage: You can establish a SEP a year after the year your contribution was for—in 1990, you can set up and contribute to a SEP for 1989. A SEP, like an IRA, can be only a defined-contribution plan, not a defined-benefit plan.

With a SEP, you can contribute 15 percent of your net self-employment income (minus your contribution), up to $30,000. The percentage winds up being 13.043 percent.

Employers can set up SEPs for their workers if they have twenty-five or fewer employees, and at least half participate. Such an SEP works like an IRA.

Unlike lump-sum distributions from a Keogh, those from a SEP don't qualify for special forward-averaging. But if you file for an extension to submit your tax return, you can also postpone making your SEP contribution.

Chapter Sixteen
ALTERNATIVE
MINIMUM TAX

If you or your tax adviser have been so clever that you've shrunk your normal taxes way, way down, the AMT may kick in.

Certain exclusions and deductions that were allowed when you figured out your taxes the regular way will now be taxed. You must calculate your taxes the regular way, then see if you've been so resourceful in avoiding taxes that you're subject to the AMT. If you are, you'll pay a higher tax.

Thanks to tax reform, there are more tax breaks that set you up for the AMT. And now the exemption from the AMT of a chunk of the income of very well-to-do people has been reduced. The exemption is normally $40,000 on a joint return, $30,000 for single people. But now, for every dollar of AMT income above $150,000 (if you're single, $112,500), you lose 25 cents of the exemption. The exemption is eliminated for joint returns at $310,000, for singles at $232,500.

Another change: The AMT rate has gone up from a flat rate of 20 percent to 21 percent. That may not seem very high. But when you recall that the highest rates this year are only 28 percent and 33 percent, you can see that the AMT will kick in sooner. It's not hard to use tax breaks to lower your overall tax rate significantly below 28 percent or 33 percent—and thus have reduced your overall tax below the trigger point, 21 percent.

Here's how you figure out the AMT:

Take your taxable income from Form 1040.

Recalculate certain items, such as for depreciation.

Add back your "tax preference" items.

Add back certain itemized deductions subject to the AMT, along with all personal exemptions and other adjustments.

You now have your "alternative minimum taxable income" (AMTI).

Subtract the exemption you're allowed ($40,000 for a married couple filing jointly, for example).

You now have the amount subject to the AMT.

Multiply it by 21 percent.

If the result is more than your regular tax, it's what you pay instead of the regular tax.

Tax breaks that set you up for the AMT are called "preferences." Some preferences are common, some rare. Among them: Any deduction you've taken for the growth in value of property (like stocks) you've given to a charity; any accelerated depreciation on real property and leased personal property, before 1987, above what would have been allowed under straight-line method; the value of real-estate depreciation deductions, after 1986, above the value of forty-year depreciation; the tax benefit of certain installment sales; the value of stock options when you exercise them; the value of mining exploration and development costs; percentage depletion allowances; intangible drilling and development costs from oil and gas properties.

To calculate your AMT income, you must also give back many tax breaks you've taken advantage of:

• Consumer interest—on credit cards, car loans, student loans—that you've deducted. For 1989, you can deduct 20 percent. For the AMT, add back those percentages. All consumer interest is prey to the AMT.

• Investment interest beyond your investment income. Under the AMT, you get no partial deduction for any excess.

• A variety of itemized deductions, including state and local income taxes, real-estate taxes, and medical expenses below 10 percent (not 7.5 percent, as with regular deductions) of your adjusted gross income.

• Any "passive" income losses you've deducted under the phaseout rules (for example, 20 percent for 1989). For the AMT, you get no breaks on passive-income losses. (Passive income comes from investments like limited partnerships.) But you can carry forward disallowed passive losses to a future year when you have offsetting passive income.

• Deductions for contributions of property (like stocks) that have gone up in value and that you've given to charity. Normally, you can claim the appreciated value of your gift. For the AMT, add back the appreciation.

• Miscellaneous itemized deductions (like employee business expenses), including those that surpassed 2 percent of your adjusted gross income.

• Interest on certain "non-essential" or "private activity" nongovernmental tax-exempt bonds issued after August 7, 1986.

• The foreign tax credit: Under the new rules, it's now limited to 90 percent of your minimum-tax liability.

If you have *any* tax-preference items, the IRS says you must submit Form 6251—even if you aren't subject to the AMT!

485 DOUBLE-CHECK THE CALCULATIONS.

Suppose you have a limited partnership that gave you a passive loss of $10,000. Included in the $10,000 might be $1,000 of accelerated depreciation—considered a tax-adjustment item. None of the $10,000 is deductible when you calculate your AMT. So the $1,000 wasn't deductible, either—and you need not add the $1,000 back into your taxable income. Yet a few computerized tax programs will do just that.

486 REMEMBER DEDUCTIONS YOU STILL CAN TAKE.

Among them: medical expenses above 10 percent of your adjusted gross income; charitable contributions, not including carryovers; casualty losses; gambling losses; investment interest to the extent of your investment income; and interest on your old mortgage balance (but not home-equity loan interest). You *can* deduct interest on a mortgage to build or rehabilitate your main home, though. But if you refinance your mortgage for more than the original balance, the interest on the additional portion of the loan isn't deductible from AMT income.

487 SUBTRACT THOSE DEDUCTIONS EVEN IF YOU DON'T ITEMIZE.

If you didn't itemize but took the standard deduction in doing your tax the regular way, you can still take allowable itemized deductions from your AMT income.

488 DON'T ADD BACK THE "EXPENSING" DEDUCTION.

The Section 179 ("expensing") deduction on new personal property, up to $10,000, isn't a tax-preference item.

489 BEWARE OF "NON-ESSENTIAL" BONDS.

Make sure your broker doesn't buy you "minimum tax," "private activity," or "non-essential" municipal bonds subject to the AMT without warning you. A tip-off: Such bonds pay higher interest than bonds not subject to the AMT.

490 TRY TO KEEP PASSIVE-LOSS DEDUCTIONS.

In 1989 you can still write off 20 percent of passive losses (earlier than August 16, 1986) against active and against portfolio income. So, if during any of these phaseout years you have large passive losses and insufficient passive gains to match them with, try especially hard to avoid the AMT—which would eliminate any passive-loss deductions altogether.

491 TRY TO KEEP HOUSING CREDITS.

Steer clear of the AMT in years when you're entitled to the low-income housing or rehabilitative-housing credit. They cannot be used to lower your AMT.

492 SHIFT INCOME AND DEDUCTIONS TO AVOID THE AMT.

Hold off giving appreciated property to a charity until a year when you'll be safe from the AMT. Avoid installment sales if they might trigger the AMT. Try to depreciate certain assets according to their usable life, not the scheduled five- to seven-year depreciation periods—so as to avoid the adjustment otherwise required by the AMT. Time the exercise of stock options, to avoid years when you may be subject to the tax.

493 SAVE DEDUCTIONS FOR A NON-AMT YEAR.

If you're planning to give appreciated property to a charity *next* year, and you may be hit by the AMT, consider making your contribution this year—along with other deductions, like for medical expenses and consumer interest. If you're subject to the AMT, you won't benefit from those deductions.

494 CONSIDER HAVING MORE INCOME SUBJECT TO THE AMT.

A 21 percent AMT is a better rate than 28 percent or 33 percent. So, consider pushing income into an AMT year—a year when you're enjoying bounteous tax breaks. Sell an asset for a gain; redeem government savings bonds; ask for a bonus earlier than scheduled.

495 REMEMBER AMT CREDITS YOU'RE ENTITLED TO.

Someday, because of accelerated depreciation, you'll have to pay more taxes. And the extra value of those stock options you exercised will finally be taxed—their value will be added to your investment when you sell. The IRS has understood this, so you may get a special AMT benefit in years when your regular tax is more than your AMT.

Recompute your AMT, adding back only certain itemized deductions, percentage depletion, tax-exempt interest, and appreciated-property charitable deductions. The difference between this AMT and the official AMT becomes a credit you can carry forward to future years, when you aren't subject to the AMT.

Appendix A
TAX RATES FOR 1989

Taxable Income	Pay . . .	Plus 1989 Tax Rates

Married-Joint Return (Two Exemptions)

0–$30,950	0	+ 15% of amount over 0
$30,950–$74,850	$ 4,642.50	+ 28% of amount over $30,950
$74,850–$177,720*	16,934.50	+ 33% of amount over $74,850
$177,720 and over	50,881.50**	+ 28% of amount over $177,720

Single Return (One Exemption)

0–$18,550	0	+ 15% of amount over 0
$18,550–$44,900	$ 2,782.50	+ 28% of amount over $18,550
$44,900–$104,330*	10,160.50	+ 33% of amount over $44,900
$104,330 and over	29,772.40**	+ 28% of amount over $104,330

*For each additional exemption, add $11,200 to taxable income.
**For each additional exemption, add $3,696 to the tax.

Taxable Income   Pay . . . Plus 1989 Tax Rates

Head of Household (One Exemption)

Taxable Income	Pay	Plus 1989 Tax Rates
0–$24,850	0	+ 15% of amount over 0
$24,850–$64,200	$3,727.50	+ 28% of amount over $24,850
$64,200–$140,010*	14,745.50	+ 33% of amount over $64,200
$140,010 and over	39,762.80**	+ 28% of amount over $140,010

The marginal tax bracket retreats to 28 percent when taxable income exceeds certain amounts—the exact amount depending upon the number of personal exemptions the taxpayer claims. The 33 percent rate is to eliminate the benefit of the 15 percent rate and personal exemptions.

Appendix B
WHAT TAXPAYERS DEDUCT

Here's what taxpayers deducted on 1987 returns—when sales-tax deductions were eliminated and medical, interest, and miscellaneous deductions were curtailed. (Source: Research Institute of America.)

Adjusted Gross Income		Medical	Taxes	Charity	Interest
$ 25,000 to	$ 30,000	$ 2,125	$ 1,818	$ 941	$ 3,605
30,000 to	40,000	2,303	2,240	1,105	4,192
40,000 to	50,000	3,042	2,807	1,130	4,928
50,000 to	75,000	4,015	3,812	1,450	5,991
75,000 to	100,000	7,292	5,684	2,135	8,217
100,000 to	200,000	16,417	9,161	3,926	11,962
200,000 to	500,000	34,869	20,233	8,320	18,371

INDEX